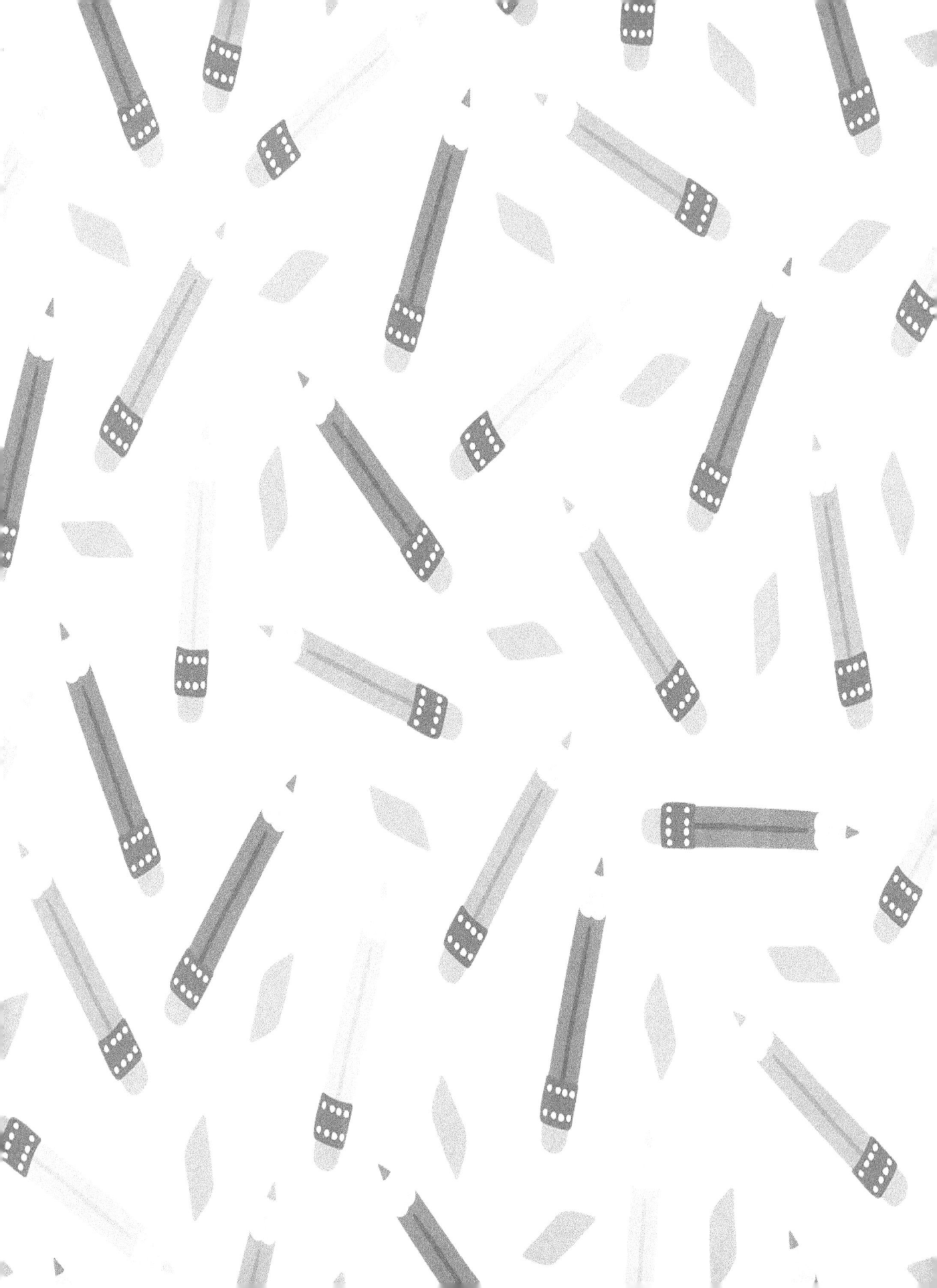

This textbook reviews the "Big 205," a list of vocabulary terms that university professors feel all college students should use in their writings and presentations. The text also reviews compound, complex and compound complex sentence structure; the type of sentence structures that will give students A's and B's. By mastering college level terms and sentence structures in this book, students will pass the threshold from high school to college!

COPYRIGHT 2017 Patsy Self Trand and Kay Lopate

All rights reserved. This publication is protected by Copyright laws. No part of this book may be reproduced, stored in a retrieval system, or transmitted in any form, or by any means, electronic, mechanical, photocopying, recording, or otherwise without prior permission of Pinecrest Street Co., and as expressly permitted by the applicable copyright statutes. Dissemination or sale of any part of this book is not permitted. Request for written permission may be obtained by writing Pinecrest Street Co., Inc., 11301 S. Dixie Hwy, Box 566684, Miami, FL 33156.

Pinecrest Street Company crest is a trademark of Pinecrest Street Company, Inc. and is registered in the U.S. Other trademarks, names, and products of other companies and institutions that may appear in the text are the property of their respective owners. Obtain written permission to use in any form these trademarks, names, and products from the respected companies and institutions.

ISBN 978-0-9995575-2-5

Library of Congress

Cover design, illustration and book design/typography: Stephanie Fernandez

Executive Editor: Mary Pope Wright

Authors: Kay Lopate and Patsy Self Trand

Published independently by Pinecrest Street Company, Inc.

Address: 11301 S. Dixie Hwy. Box 566684 Miami FL 33156

Printed in the United States

WRITE LIKE YOU ARE A COLLEGE STUDENT

LEARN COLLEGE TERMS

Vocabulary
UNIVERSITY PROFESSORS SAY ALL COLLEGE STUDENTS SHOULD KNOW

PATSY SELF TRAND, PH.D.
KAY LOPATE, PH.D.
PINECREST STREET COMPANY, INC.

IF YOU ARE GOING TO COLLEGE THEN SOUND LIKE IT

Books Published by Pinecrest Street Company, Inc.

Taking on the Challenge Series:

Making it to Graduation: Expert advice from college professors. (2017). Lopate, Kay and Trand, Patsy Self. Pinecrest Street Company, Inc.

The Official Parent Playbook: Getting your child through college. (2017) Lopate, Kay and Trand, Patsy Self. Pinecrest Street Company, Inc.

Making it in Medical School: Expert advice from college professors. (2018). Lopate, Kay and Trand, Patsy Self. Pinecrest Street Company, Inc.

Making it in Nursing School: Expert advice from college professors. (2018). Trand, Patsy Self, and Lopate, Kay. Pinecrest Street Company, Inc.

The Athletes' Playbook for College Success. (2018). Trand, Patsy Self and Lopate, Kay. Pinecrest Street Company, Inc.

Vocabulary University Professors say all College Students Should Know. (2017). Trand, Patsy Self and Lopate, Kay. Pinecrest Street Company, Inc.

College Bound Series:

30 Awesome Reading and Learning Strategies for High School Students. (2018.) Trand, Patsy Self and Lopate, Kay. Pinecrest Street Company, Inc.

Become a Great Reader and Writer in College. Book 1. (2017). Lopate, Kay and Trand, Patsy Self. Pinecrest Street Company, Inc.

Getting the Basics of Critical Thinking for College Readers and Writers. Book 2. (2018) Lopate, Kay and Trand, Patsy Self. Pinecrest Street Company, Inc.

Reading and Learning the Required College Courses in the Historical and Social Sciences. Book 3. (2017). Trand, Patsy Self and Lopate, Kay. Pinecrest Street Company, Inc.

Reading and Learning the Required College Courses in the Biological and Mathematical Sciences. Book 4 (2017). Trand, Patsy Self and Lopate, Kay. Pinecrest Street Company, Inc.

Navigating Through College Series:

30 Amazing Reading and Learning Strategies for College Students. (2017). Lopate, Kay and Trand, Patsy Self. Pinecrest Street Company, Inc.

Why I Didn't Come to Class. (2018). Trand, Patsy Self and Lopate, Kay. Pinecrest Street Company, Inc.

Capturing the Experience: My Child's First Year in College. (2018) Carpenter, Sara, Lopate, Kay and Trand, Patsy Self. Pinecrest Street Company, Inc.

Capturing the Experience: My First Year in College. (2018). Carpenter, Sara, Lopate, Kay and Trand, Patsy Self. Pinecrest Street Company, Inc.

PINECREST STREET COMPANY, INC.
Pinecrest Street Publishing

Preface for the Student, Parent and Teacher

Vocabulary University Professors say all College Students Should Know contains a list of vocabulary terms and expressions that students should know before entering college in order to feel comfortable using them in college. These terms should be in the student's oral vocabulary--when speaking in class or giving oral presentations, and these terms should also be in the student's written vocabulary when writing essays and research papers.

Vocabulary study usually falls into three categories: general terms, multiple-meaning terms and technical terms.

General Terms: General terms are mostly terms that can be used in any discipline and have a specific meaning. These terms are usually the easiest terms to learn. They may also be relationship terms and prepositions that indicate links and associations within and between sentences. An example of a general term is the word *posthumous*, meaning occurring after death. You may have studied some of these terms in Book I of The College Bound Series: *Become a Better Reader and Writer in College: Get the Basics Now.* Another general vocabulary term is the word *into*. This term is used as a preposition to link two sentences. We will explore prepositions and their role in writing later in Chapter One of this text. Another text in the College Bound Series: *Getting the Basics of Critical Thinking for College Readers and Writers. Book 2.* (2018) Lopate, Kay and Trand, Patsy Self. Pinecrest Street Company, Inc. explores the use of prepositions as they relate to critical thinking and reading comprehension.

Multi-meaning Terms: Multi-meaning terms are words with multiple meanings. These are words that may have two or more general meanings or words that have a general meaning and a technical meaning from a discipline. An example of a multi-meaning word is the word *base*. In sports it may be used as "first base, second base, third base," that is, the plates that the players run to in baseball. However, *bases* can also refer to the bottom support of a vase or tube used in chemistry. You may have studied some of these words in Book 4 *Reading and*

Learning the Required College Courses in the Biological and Mathematical Sciences.

Technical Terms: Technical terms are terms and concepts found in specific disciplines, such as *mitosis* from the field of the biology. Technical terms are featured primarily in the College Bound Series, Books 3 *Reading and Learning the Required College Courses in the Historical and Social Sciences* and Book 4 *Reading and Learning the Required College Courses in the Biological and Mathematical Sciences.* This vocabulary textbook will have only a few technical terms.

Big 205: This textbook will concentrate on all three types of vocabulary: general terms, multi-meaning terms and technical terms with only a few terms from the technical arena. The book consists of **205** words that college professors all over the country believe students should know and use in their papers, presentations and speeches. All college bound students should "take on the (challenge) which means to learn these terms and to learn them well." These terms, **unlike** the vast list of words found on the **SAT** and other college entry exams, are terms that should be used every day in college. They are terms that college professors identified to help students make the intellectual leap into the college and university arena. A main goal of this book is for all college students to use the Big 205 words in their speaking, listening and writing vocabularies!

Vocabulary University Professors say all College Students Should Know is a vocabulary workbook. Complete all the assignments in the book. Try to use these terms with family and friends as you learn them. Keep these assignments in your textbook so that your parents, teacher, and/or home school progress chart signer and approver can see your work. <u>This book meets state standards.</u>

Since the authors of this text strongly believe that word knowledge is achieved by using the newly learned words in a student's spoken, written and listening languages, the first two chapters will instruct students in the correct use of these terms in sentences. This textbook will go far beyond the safe, simple sentences used on the middle school and high school level. In addition, it will teach students how to write and speak using compound, complex and compound complex sentences. Thus, the four sentence patterns in the English language: simple sentence, compound sentence, complex sentence and compound and complex sentence patterns, will be taught exclusively in the first two chapters. You will then be expected to use these patterns in writing sentences, speeches and stories when using the newly learned terms. After reading and practicing the exercises in Chapter One, students should be able to use the newly learned words accurately in **college level** sentences and with correct punctuation. So, make sure to thoroughly understand Chapters One and Two!

Now let's begin to sound like a college student!

Table of Contents

Chapter 1	Phrases and Clauses	1
Chapter 2	Writing Awesome Sentences Like a College Graduate	15
Chapter 3	Analyze a Word	35
Chapter 4	Painting Words	43
Chapter 5	Mapping Words	51
Chapter 6	Everyday Squares	69
Chapter 7	It Is What It Is	83
Chapter 8	Taking Words to the Marketplace	97
Chapter 9	Writing Analogies	113
Chapter 10	FANFICTION	125
Chapter 11	Voctography: Visualizing Word Meanings	137
Chapter 12	Defining and Poetry	147
Bonus Chapter		152
Unit Test		154
Answer Keys		175

Chapter I

Phrases and Clauses

In this chapter you will learn to:
- Recognize prepositions
- Recognize prepositional phrases
- Recognize participles
- Recognize participial phrases
- Recognize infinitives
- Write dependent and independent clauses

Preview of the chapter:
I. Word Groups: Phrases and Clauses
    A. Phrases
        1. Prepositional
        2. Participial
        3. Infinitive
    B. Clauses
        1. Independent
        2. Dependent

Word Groups – Phrases and Clauses

Introduction

You are probably wondering why the first two chapters of a vocabulary book include phrases, clauses and sentence structure. Well, the answer is simple. If you really intend to learn new words, then you should learn how to use them correctly. Being articulate in speech and writing goes far beyond memorizing meanings of new vocabulary words and using them in short simple sentences. It means taking the core of the meaning you are trying to convey and presenting the precise essence through a strong sentence structure. The first two chapters will guide you through understanding phrases and clauses that you should use in your sentence structures. These chapters will continue by helping you to understand how to put these phrases and clauses together in order to make a strong sentence. At the end of the chapters, you will be writing compound, complex, and compound complex sentences. It is these types of sentences that will start you on your journey to writing like a college student!

The terminology in your sentence is also important. Chapters 3 through 12 will introduce you to college level vocabulary terms for your sentences. It is at this point that you will be **writing like a college student!**

Phrases and Clauses

The most basic unit of language is, of course, the word. All writings are made up of words that are grouped to give them meaning. Similarly, all speech consists of words that are grouped together to give the listener meaning. These groups are called *phrases* and *clauses*. They are combined to form sentences.

In order to understand how sentences are formed, it is essential to understand how words are formed into groups, phrases, and clauses--and how groups are formed into sentences. This understanding is essential to the skill of speaking and reading efficiently, and especially to the skill of writing with fluency and grace.

This chapter will help you to write **clear**, **error-free** sentences, the building blocks to writing effectively. Your writing skills will advance toward a college level because you will be required to use your newly acquired vocabulary words and concepts into your newly formed sentences and paragraphs. Although it is important to learn the meaning of a word, you will not "own" the word until you can use it appropriately in spoken and written language.

In order to understand how sentences are constructed, we will look at the parts of sentences –phrases and clauses – and we will then explore how they can be combined into sentences.

Phrases

A phrase is a group of words operating together without a subject and a verb. For example, take a look at the words in the boxes below. Notice that none of the phrases have a subject and verb.

at home	under the trees	to go to college
a businessman	walking home	driving a bus
after school	over the hill	without a second thought

Many modern American writers favor the use of phrases because they can make communication attractive, direct, active and vigorous. Consider the following writing below and see how the writer depends on phrases to move the action along.

They surrounded me. In complete terror, I raised my weapon and began to fire. Feeling the whistling noise as each cartridge was released toward the boys' body frame, I began to gain confidence. To win this fight is all I wanted. To leave without a scratch on my body would be a sweet victory. I fired again and again targeting another body frame, and then another. Realizing that they would recover and retaliate if I stopped for one minute, I continued to fire. Each hit took them by surprise giving me the advantage and the confidence to continue. With one final blow, my protective glasses and ear muffs fell off, and I could see the boys rolling on the ground full of laughter covered with paint. Gee, I think playing paint ball is a lot of fun. "A Paintball Game"

Chapter 1: Phrases and Clauses | 5

    This is good stuff and worth trying. Did you notice how the phrases create interest? This is exactly what you want to do in your writing. To begin to write like this simply means that you must go through two steps. The first step in moving our own ideas into phrases is to be aware that there are three kinds of phrases: prepositional phrases, participial phrases and infinitive phrases.

Prepositional Phrases

    Prepositional phrases are the most common sort of phrases. The prepositional phrase is composed of the preposition, its object and modifiers of the object. A prepositional phrase begins with a preposition.

    Here is a partial list of some of the most common prepositions. Study the list. For Practice Exercise One, recreate the list without looking back at the list below.

List of Commonly used Prepositions

after	upon	following
above	with	across
against	without	behind
because	at	beyond
between	including	except
of	until	around
from	despite	near
into	among	during
like	for	but
on	on	beneath
past	by	down
regarding	over	below
through	before	as
towards	since	so
until	along	

Vocabulary University Professors say all College Students Should Know

Activity

Practice Exercise 1: Test your knowledge of prepositions. Without looking back at the list of prepositions, use the boxes in the matrix to write all the prepositions you can remember. You might want to cover the list of prepositions with a sheet of paper to help you avoid looking at the list. Then check back for any you may have missed and complete the matrix.

Practice Exercise 2: Look back at the paragraph on "A Paint Ball Game." List in the space provided all the prepositions found in the paragraph.

_____   _____   _____

_____   _____   _____

_____   _____   _____

Prepositional phrases are often used to replace clauses and to give the clause a more direct and active meaning. Read the examples below to get a better idea of how the prepositional phrase enhances a clause.

Example 1
a) The water was cold.
   <u>Because of the cold water</u>, the children stayed on the beach.

b) The children stayed on the beach.
   The children avoided the cold water <u>by staying on the beach</u>.

Practice Exercise 3: Build the simple sentence. Give the sentences below a direct and active meaning by adding a preposition or prepositional phrase. Use Example 1 above to help you write your sentence. The first one is done for you.

a) I like early dismissal from school.

<u>Because I like early dismissal from school, I was extremely excited about going to school today.</u>

b) I listen to music on my lunch breaks.

_____

c) It will be easy for you to find.

_____

d) I found a doll.

_____

e) Time is slipping by.

_____

Participial Phrases

A participial phrase is a word group consisting of a present participle which is the "_ing" form of a verb and acts like an adjective, that is, describes a person, place or thing. The present participial phrases are most commonly used in present-day writing. For example, in the sentence, "The student riding the skate board is my neighbor," the phrase "riding the skate board" is a participial phrase and it describes the student. A participial phrase can also include a past participle which is an -ed, -d, -en form of a verb. This past participial phrase also serves as an adjective. An example of a past participial phrase can be seen in the sentence, "Broken windows are results of strong winds during hurricanes." The past participial phrase is "broken windows," which describes the results of strong winds during hurricanes.

Activity

Exercise 4:   In the earlier selection on page 4, "A Paint Ball Game," try to find the participial phrases and write them below.

_____   _____   _____   _____

Participles can also be used as a noun. When they are used this way they are called gerunds. Below are examples of participles used as a noun.

1. <u>Mary's being here</u> did not hurt us at all. [Phrase is subject of the verb "hurt."]
2. I hate <u>taking exams.</u> [phrase is object of the verb "hate."]

Infinitive Phrases

This is a familiar type of prepositional phrase. This phrase is made using "to" plus the root form of the verb. Examples of infinitives are "to dream," "to run," "to jump," and "to play." Now go back to "A Paintball Game" on page 4 and find the infinitives in the paragraph.

Activity

Exercise 5: - Find five infinitives in "A Paint Ball Game" and write them below.

_____   _____   _____   _____   _____

Exercise 6: Underline the phrases in the following sentences. Then on the line beneath the sentence, identify the type of phrase: prepositional, participial or infinitive phrase.

1. To get better grades, he studied more.
_____

2. We work to earn a living.
_____

3. I love cooking meals for us.
_____

4. The children fled the old house screaming that they had seen a ghost.
_____

5. His picture hangs above the fireplace.
_____

6. Without her help, we would have been lost.
_____

7. Because of his kindness and consideration, he won the scholarship.
_____

8. He works hard to earn a better salary and to support his family.
_____

9. Practicing all day long, helped him earn a spot on the football team.
_____

10. My sister is the girl wearing a pink suit.
_____

11. As soon as it got dark, they went home.
_____

12. I love cooking meals for us.
_____

13. He works hard to earn a better salary.
_____

14. His picture hangs above the fireplace.
_____

15. She threw the ball at me.
_____

16. You can see the pain on the old man's face from working all day long.
_____

17. His participating here has helped many children learn the importance of good heath.
_____

18. Jogging to work helped Diana stay healthy.
_____

19. He loves to sing in the shower.
_____

20. Dancing all night long caused the young student to oversleep.
_____

Clauses

A clause is a group of words that have a subject and a verb; a clause can be either independent or it can be dependent. An independent clause stands alone and does not need an additional clause to make it a sentence. It is a sentence. A dependent clause is an incomplete sentence and needs an independent clause to make it a complete sentence. When a dependent clause stands alone and is presented as a sentence, professors mark it wrong and label it as a "fragment." Confused? Well let's look at each clause one at a time, and the difference will be clear.

Independent Clauses

An independent clause, also known as a main clause, expresses a complete and independent idea. It can stand alone as a simple sentence. For example, take the sentence, "I sing." This clause can stand along as a sentence, a simple sentence. Now let's look at another sentence, "He loves football." Again this clause is independent and is a simple sentence. Remember, a sentence expresses a complete thought and has a subject and a verb.

Dependent Clauses

A dependent clause, also known as a subordinate clause, expresses an incomplete and dependent idea. It cannot stand alone as a sentence. It **depends** on an independent clause (simple sentence) to complete its meaning to become a sentence. Independent clauses are prepositional phrases, participial phrases and infinitives. Below are examples of dependent clauses.

    on the hill   in the house   to run   joining the team

Notice that although these are clauses, none of them can serve as a sentence by themselves. They need an additional statement, an independent clause, to complete the idea of a sentence. It is these clauses that your professors will mark as "fragments."

Now, let's look at an example of a dependent clause versus an independent clause. If someone were to rush into a classroom and shout, "because the school's on fire," we would gape at him or her and wonder what he or she was talking about. However, if someone were to rush in and shout, "Everyone must evacuate immediately [independent clause and simple sentence] because the school is on fire [dependent clause and prepositional phrase], then we would understand and leave the room quickly.

In our speech we use dependent clauses all the time and when we write sometimes we do the same. Most commonly, we do this by taking an ordinary independent clause, a simple sentence, and follow it by another sentence which is a dependent clause assuming that the subject, verb or complete thought will continue into that next sentence. Each sentence we write must have a subject, verb, and a complete thought. This sentence is an independent clause.

Activity

Exercise 7: Below are dependent clauses (DC). They are prepositional phrases, participial phrases and infinitive phrases. In **front** of the dependent clause, write an independent clause (IC) to make the clause into a sentence.

Sample: because the school is on fire.
Sentence: Everyone must evacuate immediately because the school is on fire.

1. until we meet again
Sentence:_____.

2. to run
Sentence:_____

3. singing in the shower
Sentence:_____

Exercise 8 In the following sentences, mark the underlined groups of words as IC for independent clause or DC for dependent clause.

1. <u>We listened to music</u> while we drove home.

2. <u>As soon as it was dark</u>, they went home.

3. If we get up early enough, <u>we will be able to watch the sunrise.</u>

4. They work hard <u>so that they may party well.</u>

5. Whenever I hear her voice, <u>I think of home.</u>

6. Mary went to the dance <u>because she wanted to meet her best friend.</u>

7. The weather was warm <u>during the night.</u>

8. The teacher was tired <u>so she gave the students seat assignments.</u>

9. Martha got a new car <u>since the old one continuously broke down on her.</u>

10. <u>We went to all the stores</u> trying to find the dress.

Chapter 2

Writing Awesome Sentences Like a College Graduate

In this chapter you will learn to:
- Write a correctly punctuated complex sentence
- Write a correctly punctuated compound sentence
- Write a correctly punctuated compound complex sentence
- Immediately recognize sentence fragments and know how to fix them
- Immediately recognize sentence punctuation errors and know how to fix them
- Write and speak like a college student by using advanced sentence structures

Preview the chapter
I. Combining Sentences

   The Simple Sentence

   The Less Than Simple Sentence

   The Compound Sentence (Coordination)

   The Complex Sentence (Subordination)

   The Compound-Complex Sentence (Coordination and Subordination)

   Sentence Combining Exercises

   Combining Sentences to Form Paragraphs

Introduction

Now that we understand how words are grouped into phrases and clauses, we can proceed to understanding how grouping phrases, clauses and sentences together will eventually give you a robust sentence that is full of detail, interest and fluency. In Chapter One we discussed that the first step of moving your ideas on paper is through the use of phrases and clauses. This chapter will discuss and identify step two of how to combine sentences to advance and perfect the message you are trying to convey.

In the English language, there are only four basic types of sentences in English. Any idea or related group of ideas can be organized into a simple sentence, a compound sentence, a complex sentence, or a compound-complex sentence.

Let's now look at those four sentence patterns and how sentences can be created from the word groups we have already studied.

The Simple Sentence

A simple sentence is a group of words which contains a subject and a verb and which expresses a complete and independent idea. For example let's look at the sentences:

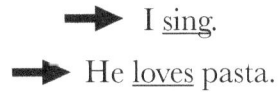
➡ I <u>sing</u>.
➡ He <u>loves</u> pasta.

A simple sentence is called an independent clause (**IC**). Both simple sentences and independent clauses can stand alone.

Activity

Exercise 1: Write three simple sentences of your own. Draw an arrow to the subject of each sentence and underline the verb of each sentence as shown in the examples above.

1._____

2._____

3._____

Compound Sentences

A compound sentence is made up of two simple sentences (independent clauses) which are joined together to show the coordination of the two main ideas of the simple sentences. Two independent clauses can be joined by a comma and a coordination conjunction, or they can be joined by a semicolon if no conjunction is needed or desired.

Example:
I like Sarah, but I hate her brother.
I like Sarah; I hate her brother

Pattern:

IC	,for	IC
	,and	
	,nor	
	,but	
	,or	
	,yet	
	,so	
	;	

These coordinating conjunctions that combine two sentences together (two independent clauses) can be remembered by the acronym: FANBOYS. The first letter in the word FANBOYS represents the coordinating conjunctions for, and, nor, but, or, yet, so. These conjunctions that combine two sentences are punctuated with a comma in front of the conjunction. The semicolon also serves as punctuation. So, if you want to join two independent clauses (two simple sentences) together, make sure you combine with a comma plus one of the FANBOYS or with a semi colon. Two sentences or independent clauses together as one sentence are called a **compound sentence**.

Example:
I had fish for lunch.
Guess what my mother served for dinner.
Compound Sentence: I had fish for lunch, so guess what my mother served for dinner.

Activity

Exercise 2: Combine the two sentences below making them into a compound sentence. Follow the example on the previous page.

1. Alice did not particularly care for the salad dressing offered.
    She made another choice.

Compound sentence_____

2. Those who knew him said he was reserved.
    He introduced himself to everyone at the party.

Compound sentence_____

3. George can buy new skis during the summer sales.
  He can polish his old ones and use them for another year.

Compound sentence _____

4. He's a jolly good fellow.
    He's a jolly good fellow.

Compound sentence_____

5. Marie never fully accepted the gravity of her father's condition.
    Did she grasp his illness as a terminal one?

Compound sentence_____

6. John hasn't called in sick.
We are quite worried about him.

Compound sentence_____

7. I studied hard for the exam.
I received a very high grade.

Compound sentence_____

8. Steve plays the saxophone.

May sings folk songs.

Compound sentence_____

9. The sun was shining.

It was raining.

Compound sentence_____

10. Larry is the best player on the team.

He was ill the day of the big game.

Compound sentence_____

11. The final was scheduled for today.

The professor is absent.

Compound sentence_____

12. The nurse gave the child some medicine.

It was delicious.

Compound sentence_____

13. Bertha loves Clint Eastwood.

She goes to all of his movies.

Compound sentence_____

14. Sue cleaned the boat.

Mike secured the rigging.

Compound sentence_____

15. George was playing the tuba.

Mary was not listening.

Compound sentence_____

The Complex Sentence

A complex sentence is a sentence made up of an independent clause (IC) and a dependent clause (DC). As an independent clause, it can stand alone, but a dependent clause cannot stand alone. By itself, a dependent clause would be a sentence fragment. It is usually dependent because it contains a word that makes it dependent. These words are prepositions, participles and infinitives. These words form prepositional phrases, participial phrases and infinitives.

Examples:

I took my car to the garage because it was not running well.

In this example, "because it was not running well," is a prepositional phrase and "I took my car to the garage" is an independent clause or simple sentence. Therefore, a complex sentence is a prepositional phrase, participial phrase or infinitive attached to a simple sentence (independent clause).

Because it was not running well, I took my car to the garage. Notice the punctuation at the end of the dependent clause. If the dependent clause begins the sentence, then at the end of the dependent clause place a comma, then continue with the independent clause.

Pattern:

IC DC
DC, IC

Example:

It was late.

I went straight home.

Complex sentence: "Because it was late, I went straight home." One of the independent clauses (sentences) was changed to a prepositional phrase to make the sentence a complex sentence. Notice that a comma was added before the independent clause and after the prepositional phrase.

However, if you write the sentence, "I went straight home because it was late," then you do not need to add a comma because the prepositional phrase comes after the independent clause.

You can turn an independent clause (sentence) into a dependent clause by making it a preposition, participial or infinitive to the independent clause. You may want to change the sentences into these phrases to explain a relationship more clearly.

Example:

Mary was playing the piano.

The music teacher was not listening.

Complex sentence: Although Mary was playing the piano, the music teacher was not listening.

Or

The music teacher was not listening although Mary was playing the piano.

Activity

Exercise 3

Read the two independent clauses below. Change one of the independent clauses into one of the dependent clauses (prepositional phrase, participial phrase, infinitive phrase) and then write a complex sentence. Use the model above to guide you.

1. It was raining.

The sun was shining brightly.

Complex sentence_____

2. I finished working.

I took a nap.

Complex sentence_____

3. Mark has a fever.

Please don't visit him.

Complex sentence_____

Chapter 2: Writing Awesome Sentences Like a College Graduate | 23

4. Let's light the fireplace.

It's cold tonight.

Complex sentence_____

5. The teacher would not leave.

The last child left.

Complex sentence_____

6. It is raining.

The children have umbrellas.

Complex sentence_____

7. The boys are in the park.

Their parents are at work.

Complex sentence_____

8. People used more fuel than usual.

It was the coldest winter in a century.

Complex sentence_____

9. The famous singer sang his most popular songs.

Thousands of people applauded.

Complex sentence_____

10. Mary won't show up.

John says so.

Complex sentence_____

11. People are happy.

The stock market is going up.

Complex sentence_____

12. We watched.

The sky turned gray.

Complex sentence_____

13. Her mother took the doll.

The little girl cried.

Complex sentence_____

14. We worked on the car.

The girls watched T.V.

Complex sentence_____

15. I went to see "Hamilton."

I am a big fan of the theatre.

Complex sentence_____

Now write three complex sentences on your own.

1._____

2._____

3._____

The Compound Complex Sentence

A compound complex sentence is a combination of a compound and a complex sentence. It is made up of two independent clauses: IC – FANBOYS or, – IC and one dependent clause DC. So you already know the model for the compound complex sentence! It is just putting the two structures together.

	Clause	Punctuation	Clause	Punctuation	Clause
Option 1	IC	**FANBOYS**	IC	none	DC
Option 2	IC	none	DC	comma	IC
Option 3	DC	comma	IC	**FANBOYS**	IC

Example:

Option 1: I have enjoyed living in the city, but I prefer the country side because it is peaceful and quiet.

Option 2: It is nice to travel because you learn a lot, and your view on life will change.

Option 3: Since I need to finish my homework, I told my friends I could not play, and they became very angry.

Activity

Exercise 4: Using commas, FANBOYS and semicolons as appropriate, combine the following groups of simple sentences into compound complex sentences. Remember to place a comma before your coordinating conjunctions (FANBOYS) and a comma after the dependent clause. The first sentence is done for you.

1. It was Friday the thirteenth.
Margaret was scared all day.
Bob scoffed at the silly superstitions of his friends.

Compound Complex sentence: <u>Because it was Friday the thirteenth, Margaret was scared all day, but Bob scoffed at the silly superstitions of his friends.</u>

2. Winter snow in the Rockies gets very deep.
Avoiding snow drifts becomes imperative.
One must exercise caution.

Compound Complex sentence_____

3. Joe bought a new car.
He had brake problems the week after he purchased it.
He was furious.

Compound Complex sentence_____

4. The baby cried steadily.
His mother came home.
The babysitter heaved a sigh of relief.

Complex Compound sentence_____

5. We go to Knottsberry Farm.
We wanted delicious and fresh strawberries.
We picked the fruit to our hearts' content.

Complex Compound sentence_____

6. John runs.

He drinks Gatorade.

He does warm up exercises.

Compound Complex sentence_____

7. You want to pick up your paycheck.

You must come to the office on the fifth floor.

Proper identification must be presented.

Compound Complex sentence_____

8. Jill leaves.

I will call you.

Don't wait up for my call.

Compound Complex sentence_____

9. Gloria enjoys playing tennis.

She rarely has time for the sport.

She is carrying a full course load at the university.

Compound Complex sentence_____

10. It rained so much.

The pond behind our house overflowed.

Our kitchen floor was damaged.

Compound Complex sentence_____

11. I will not give you any apple pie.

You eat every bit of your dinner.

I mean what I say.

Compound Complex sentence_____

12. Miguel had a strong personality.

Everyone in the village liked him.

He was frequently called upon to settle disputes.

Compound Complex sentence_____

13. Douglas treads.

No man dares to walk.

He frequently gets into trouble.

Compound Complex sentence_____

14. You begin the College Entrance Exam.

Please put your name in the boxes at the top of the page.

Read the directions very carefully.

Compound Complex sentence_____

15. Shooting deer is not one of Bill's favorite sports.

He thought of declining the invitation.

He heard most of his friends would participate in the hunting expedition.

Compound Complex_____

Now you write three compound complex sentences on your own.

1._____

2._____

3._____

The Four Sentence Patterns Chart

Clause Type +	Puncuation +	Clause Type	= Type of Sentence
Independent clause + (Simple sentence)	no punctuation +	none	= Simple Sentence
Independent clause + (Simple sentence)	FANBOYS + ,for ,and ,nor ,but ,or ,yet ,so ;	Independent clause (Simple sentence)	= Compound (Sentence)
Independent clause + (Simple sentence)	no punctuation +	Dependent Clause (Prepositional phrase) (Participial phrase) (Infinitive phrase)	= Complex Sentence

Clause	Puncuation	Clause	Puncuation	Clause
Independent clause + (Simple sentence)	FANBOYS + ,for ,and ,nor ,but ,or ,yet ,so ;	Independent clause + (Simple sentence)	no punctuation +	Dependent clause = (Prepositional phrase) (Participial phrase) (Infinitive phrase)

= Compound Complex Sentence

Dependent clause + (Prepositional phrase) (Participial phrase) (Infinitive phrase)	comma [,] +	Independent clause + (Simple Sentence)	FANBOYS + ,for ,and ,nor ,but ,or ,yet ,so ;	Independent clause = (Simple Sentence)

= Compound Complex Sentence

Tear and Carry
The Four Sentence Patterns Chart

Rip this page out of your book and keep it with you when you continue on to the next chapters.

You will have to write **college level** sentences with your newly acquired words. These sentences will be basically compound sentences, complex sentences and compound complex sentences. A few simple sentences will be allowed. Punctuation must be correct!

I	Simple Sentence	=	IC (Independent Clause)
II	Compound Sentence	=	IC + FANBOYS + IC
III	Complex Sentence	=	IC + no punctuation + DC (Dependent Clause)
		=	DC + Comma [,] + IC
IV	Compound Complex Sentence	=	IC + FANBOYS + IC + no punctuation + DC
		=	DC + Comma [,] + IC + FANBOYS + DC

NOW YOU CAN WRITE SENTENCES LIKE A COLLEGE STUDENT!

GIVE YOURSELF A TREAT!

NOW LET'S MAKE SURE WE USE COLLEGE LEVEL TERMINOLOGY AND CONCEPTS IN OUR SENTENCES!!!

MAKE THIS COLLEGE LEVEL COMPLETE.

Introduction to Chapters 3-12

You just finished learning how to write advanced level sentences. The remaining chapters have the terminology you will learn to match your level of sentences. These words are words that most college professors expect students to know when entering college. Furthermore, these words are not like the words on high stake tests like the SAT and ACT (sometimes when you use them, nobody really understands you!) These are words that you must use to make your writing precise, meaningful and polished. In the rest of the textbook you will learn words that should be part of your college vocabulary. To learn these words, you will use some critical thinking skills, prior knowledge, background knowledge, and the plain old tactic of looking it up the dictionary, thesaurus or a textbook's glossary.

Chapter 3

Analyze a Word

In this chapter you will learn to:

- Understand the meaning of the words and concepts listed below:

gratuitous	inhibition	posthumous	omnipotent
omniscient	deductive	inductive	benevolence
fortuitous	empathy	apathy	autonomy
memoirs	maxim	biofeedback	jocularity
decimate	assumption	transient	etymology

- Know how to use these words in sentences.

Preview the chapter

I. Learn to analyze a word

    a. parts of speech

    b. meaning

    c. meaning of word parts

II. Using the terms in sentences

    a. compound sentences

    b. complex sentences

    c. compound complex sentences

    d. simple sentences

III. Practice Exercises A and B

Define This Chapter's Vocabulary Words

1. _____
2. _____
3. _____
4. _____
5. _____
6. _____
7. _____
8. _____
9. _____
10. _____
11. _____
12. _____
13. _____
14. _____
15. _____
16. _____
17. _____
18. _____
19. _____
20. _____

Word Parts

It is easy to remember the meaning of some words if you know some of the familiar parts that make up the words. Although you may not know the full meaning of a word, you may be able to infer the meaning of the word, by using the meanings of word parts (prefix, root, or suffix). It is important to be able to analyze a word by recognizing familiar word parts. We recommend for students to keep a list of prefixes, roots, and suffixes with their associated meanings. You will begin to find patterns and realize that word part meanings basically stay the same regardless of the word in which they appear. In the following chart, you will be asked to define the word part.

Part of Speech

Did you ever try to use a term that you know the meaning of but cannot fit it in a sentence correctly? Well, chances are that if you know the part of speech (noun, adjective, adverb, adjective, etc.) to which the word belongs, then the task of using the word correctly in a sentence is that much easier. Completing the word chart on page 38 will help you in this task.

Dictionary Meaning

Looking up a word in the dictionary is a simple thing to do, so do it. You do need to know the other elements that the chart asks for, but the dictionary meaning is priceless.

Word History

Not only are word parts important to the meaning of words, but also to their origin! But chances are that if you do not know the meaning of the word, then you probably do not know the word origin or history. So when you look up a word in the dictionary, make sure you know more than the meaning, but also make sure to read the history of the word. That should help you understand the meaning.

Activity

Using the vocabulary words from this chapter, complete the chart on page 39. Make sure you write in the part of speech (noun, adjective etc.) and the definitions. In addition, write in the definition of the word part -prefix, suffix or base word. Use the Analyze a Word chart provided to write in your information for the list of this chapter's vocabulary words listed below.

gratuitous	inhibition	posthumous	omnipotent
omniscient	deductive	inductive	benevolence
fortuitous	empathy	apathy	autonomy
memoirs	maxim	biofeedback	jocularity
decimate	assumption	transient	etymology

Analyze A Word Chart

Word	Part of Speech	Meaning of Word Part(s)	Dictionary Meaning	Word History

Practice Exercise A: Match the vocabulary word on the left with its definition in the right column. Place the correct definition in the space provided.

1. _____posthumous   a. costing nothing; unnecessary and unwarranted
2. _____deductive   b. a feeling or belief that prevents spontaneity
3. _____inductive   c. unlimited power; all powerful
4. _____fortuitous   d. all powerful
5. _____autonomy   e. using general principles to draw specific statements
6. _____gratuitous   f. using specific statements to draw general principles
7. _____ empathy   g. happening after death
8. _____ apathy   h. a good thing that occurred by no apparent cause
9. _____ memoirs   i. complete understanding of another's feeling or situation
10. _____ omnipotent   j. without feeling or emotion, of another's situation
11. _____ maxim   k. independence or freedom; self-government
12. _____ biofeedback   l. an account of the author's personal experiences
13. _____ decimate   m. fun; humorist
14. _____inhibition   n. something that is believed to be true without proof
15. _____ assumption   o. the study or the origins of parts of words
16. _____benevolence   p. the act of doing good; showing kindness
17._____ jocularity   q. giving information to a person about his/her voluntary
18._____ transient   and involuntary bodily processes
19._____etymology   r. staying in a place for only a short period of time
20._____omniscient   s. killing or removing every ten
                                     t. a saying that is widely expected

Practice Exercise B:

Write four simple sentences, four compound sentences, four complex sentences and four compound complex sentences using the words you learned in this chapter. You decide which word you prefer to use in which sentence structure.

Simple Sentences

1_____
2_____
3_____
4_____

Compound Sentences

1_____
2_____
3_____
4_____

Complex Sentences

1_____
2_____
3_____
4_____

Compound Complex Sentences

1_____
2_____
3_____
4_____

Chapter 4

Painting Words

In this chapter you will learn to:
- Understand the meaning of the words and concepts listed below:

quixotic	boon	aghast	insidious
flaunt	haphazard	infer	meander
intrepid	minutiae	advocate	preposterous
remorseful	longevity	ambiguity	ambivalence
melancholy	penury	nonchalant	discord

- Use these terms to show intensity or loss of strength in expression
- Use the terms in college level sentences

Preview the chapter

I. Synonyms for the learning words for this chapter.

II. Relationships between the learning words and some of the synonyms

III. Practice exercise A and B

Define This Chapter's Vocabulary Words

1. _____
2. _____
3. _____
4. _____
5. _____
6. _____
7. _____
8. _____
9. _____
10. _____
11. _____
12. _____
13. _____
14. _____
15. _____
16. _____
17. _____
18. _____
19. _____
20. _____

Introduction

What is meant by painting words?

The English language has many words that have the same or similar meaning, but the meanings of some of these words vary in intensity, from more intensity or less intensity. For example, let's look at the word "glad," meaning happy. The word "cheerful" has a similar meaning, but it is a more intense, happy feeling than glad. Thus, words may be related in terms of synonyms, but there is a range of meaning within the general meaning of a group of associated synonyms that either intensifies or decreases in intensity. As a college student, you need a vocabulary that is not trite and that encompasses a range of words that describe complex and simple situations. Below is a paint swap, similar to the ones you will find at a paint store, but in this exercise, instead of deciding on the exact intensity of color for a wall, you will decide on the exact intensity of the word to match the precise meaning you are trying to convey. Knowing how to choose the best word is helpful in all your classes at the university and especially in your English, Humanities and History classes. Make sure you learn these words well because these university/college courses are required throughout the country.

Activity

The first word to paint is done for you:

→ melancholy   depressed   miserable

The vocabulary word, "melancholy," is from our learning list for this chapter. The other two words that were placed on the row are words that increase the definition and intensity of the word melancholy. You will find the learning words are already provided for you in the chart. Complete the chart by increasing the intensity of the word. Three of our learning words for this chapter are high intensity, so you will need to find a less intense word for those columns.

→   Increase intensity of the feeling or thought the words convey   →

Melancholy	Depressed	Miserable
Nonchalant		
Boon		
Meander		
Longevity		
Ambiguity		
Ambivalence		
Preposterous		
		Penury
Advocate		
		aghast
discord		
Minutiae		
infer		
Flaunt		
Haphazard		
Insidious		
Intrepid		
		Remorseful
Quixotic		

Practice Exercise A

Match the word with the definition:

1. _____ quixotic   a. overwhelming shock; fright
2. _____ flaunt   b. done in a way that has not been planned
3. _____ intrepid   c. treacherous; sneaky
4. _____ remorseful   d. slow walk or journey
5. _____ melancholy   e. small or trivia details
6. _____ boon   f. disagreement
7. _____ aghast   g. romantic behavior; idealistic
8. _____ insidious   h. outrageous; absurd
9. _____ haphazard   i. fearless; dauntless
10. _____ infer   j. the length of a person's or animal's life
11. _____ meander   k. understood in more than one way; uncertain
12. _____ minutiae   l. calm and unconcerned; indifferent
13. _____ advocate   m. to show off; to display on parade
14. _____ preposterous   n. feeling gloomy or sadness
15. _____ longevity   o. to support or speak in favor of something
16. _____ ambiguity   p. guilt; regret
17. _____ ambivalence   q. a gift or favor from someone
18. _____ penury   r. poverty; penniless
19. _____ nonchalant   s. to come to a conclusion based on evidence
20. _____ discord   t. conflict of ideas; contradiction; uncertain

Practice Exercise B

Write one sentence that includes the pair of words listed.

Advocate, empathy

1._____

Benevolence, longevity

2._____

Meander, ambivalent

3._____

Nonchalant, apathy

4._____

Omniscient, discord

5._____

Intrepid, minutiae

6._____

Boon, flaunt

7._____

Preposterous, insidious

8._____

Quixotic, Haphazard

9._____

Aghast, discord

10._____

Chapter 5

Mapping Words

In this chapter you will learn to:

•   Understand the meaning of the words and concepts listed below:

epicure	cognition	astute	visage
perennial	narcissism	guttural	somatic
omnipotent	secular	consensus	sporadic
modes of persuasion -	latent	plagiarism	subjugate
(pathos, logos, ethos)	wit	introvert	
	amenable	panacea	
	epicure	paragon	

Preview of the chapter:

1. What is a word map?

2. What is a word map used for?

3. Why do we need word maps?

4. How do word maps help us in writing?

2. Word Map Components

    a. Part of speech

    b. Antonyms

    c. Synonyms

    d. Characteristics or examples of words

Define This Chapter's Vocabulary Words

1. _____
2. _____
3. _____
4. _____
5. _____
6. _____
7. _____
8. _____
9. _____
10. _____
11. _____
12. _____
13. _____
14. _____
15. _____
16. _____
17. _____
18. _____
19. _____
20. _____

Introduction

What is a word map?

A word map is a visual display that shows relationships within elements of a word. They extend knowledge, explain concepts and portray a visual meaning and usage of a word.

What is a word map used for?

Word maps are used as a communication tool to depict knowledge, concepts, ideas and relationships in the form of a cognitive organizer.

Why do we need word maps?

Word maps help us quickly understand the meaning of words. They are an effective tool that enables a student to understand the meaning and usage of a word at a glance.

How do word maps help us with writing?

Word maps give us information that is necessary to correctly use the term in sentences and paragraphs. These maps guide the learner's thinking about word usage and its relationship to other information in the writing.

Activity

On the next five pages you will find four maps per page. Fill out these maps. You will need a dictionary and a thesaurus. In the appropriate boxes, fill in the antonyms, synonyms, characteristics or examples, and part of speech.

Directions: Insert into boxes

Upper left- part of speech
Lower left- antonym

Upper right- characteristic or examples
Lower right- synonym

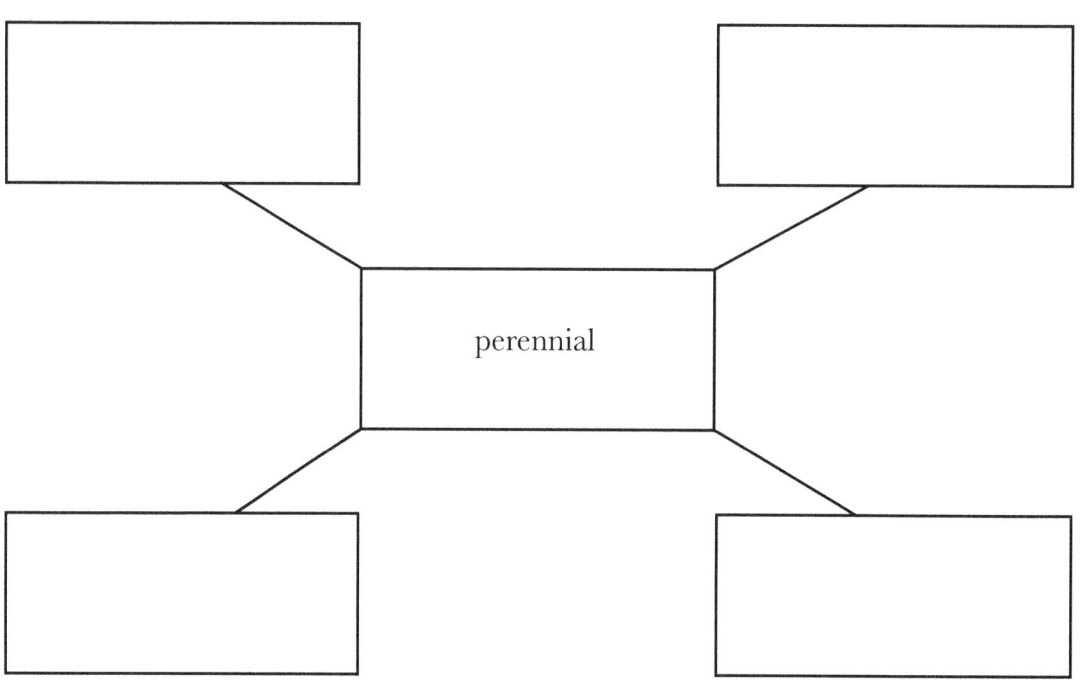

Chapter 5: Mapping Words | 55

Directions: Insert into boxes

Upper left- part of speech
Lower left- antonym

Upper right- characteristic or examples
Lower right- synonym

Modes of persuasion

omnipotent

Directions: Insert into boxes

Upper left- part of speech
Lower left- antonym

Upper right- characteristic or examples
Lower right- synonym

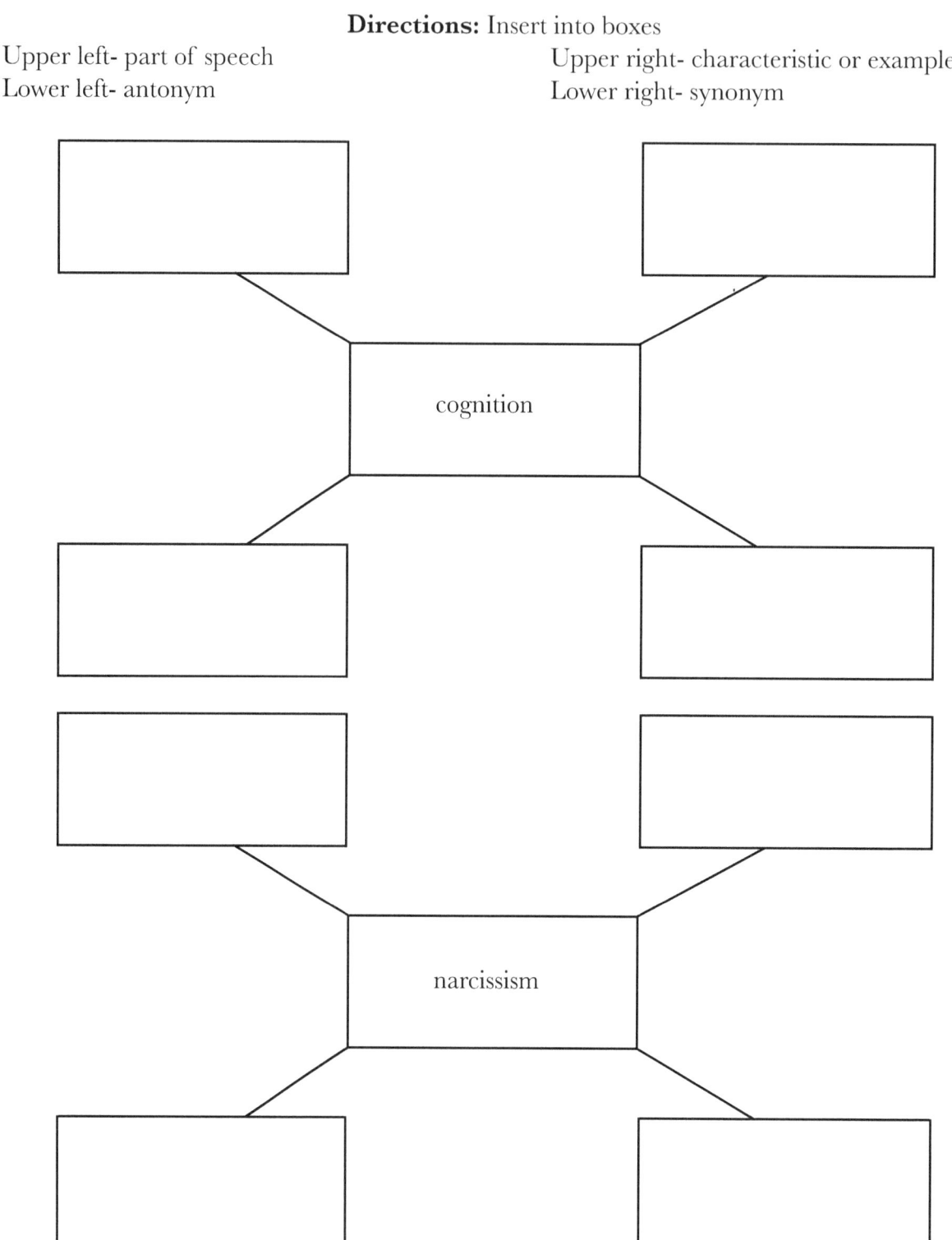

Chapter 5: Mapping Words | 57

Directions: Insert into boxes

Upper left- part of speech
Lower left- antonym

Upper right- characteristic or examples
Lower right- synonym

secular

Latent

58 | Vocabulary University Professors say all College Students Should Know

Directions: Insert into boxes

Upper left- part of speech
Lower left- antonym

Upper right- characteristic or examples
Lower right- synonym

wit

amenable

Chapter 5: Mapping Words | 59

Directions: Insert into boxes

Upper left- part of speech
Lower left- antonym

Upper right- characteristic or examples
Lower right- synonym

astute

Consensus

Vocabulary University Professors say all College Students Should Know

Directions: Insert into boxes

Upper left- part of speech
Lower left- antonym

Upper right- characteristic or examples
Lower right- synonym

guttural

plagiarism

Chapter 5: Mapping Words | 61

Directions: Insert into boxes

Upper left- part of speech
Lower left- antonym

Upper right- characteristic or examples
Lower right- synonym

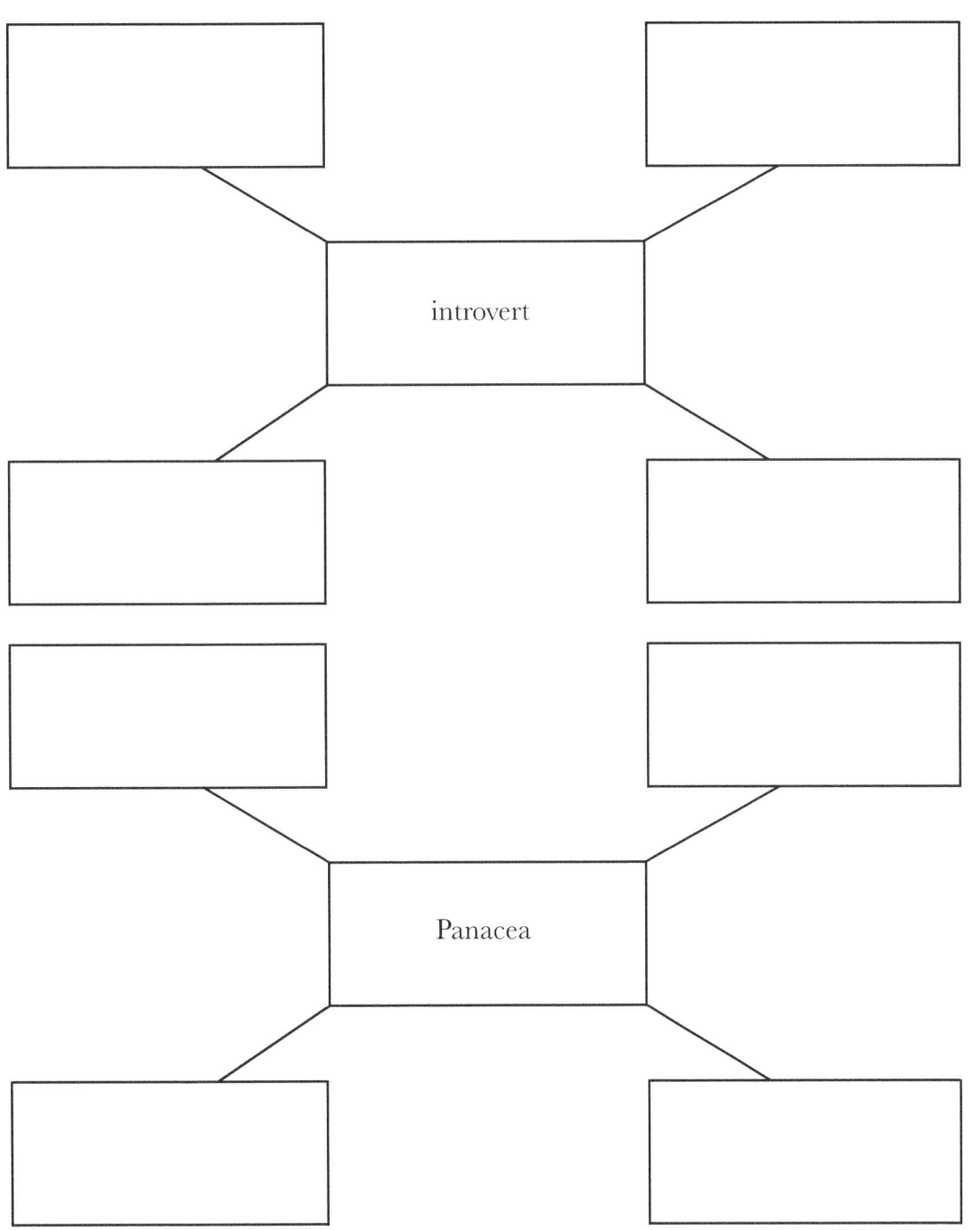

Directions: Insert into boxes

Upper left- part of speech
Lower left- antonym

Upper right- characteristic or examples
Lower right- synonym

paragon

visage

Chapter 5: Mapping Words | 63

Directions: Insert into boxes

Upper left- part of speech
Lower left- antonym

Upper right- characteristic or examples
Lower right- synonym

somatic

Sporadic

Directions: Insert into boxes

Upper left- part of speech
Lower left- antonym

Upper right- characteristic or examples
Lower right- synonym

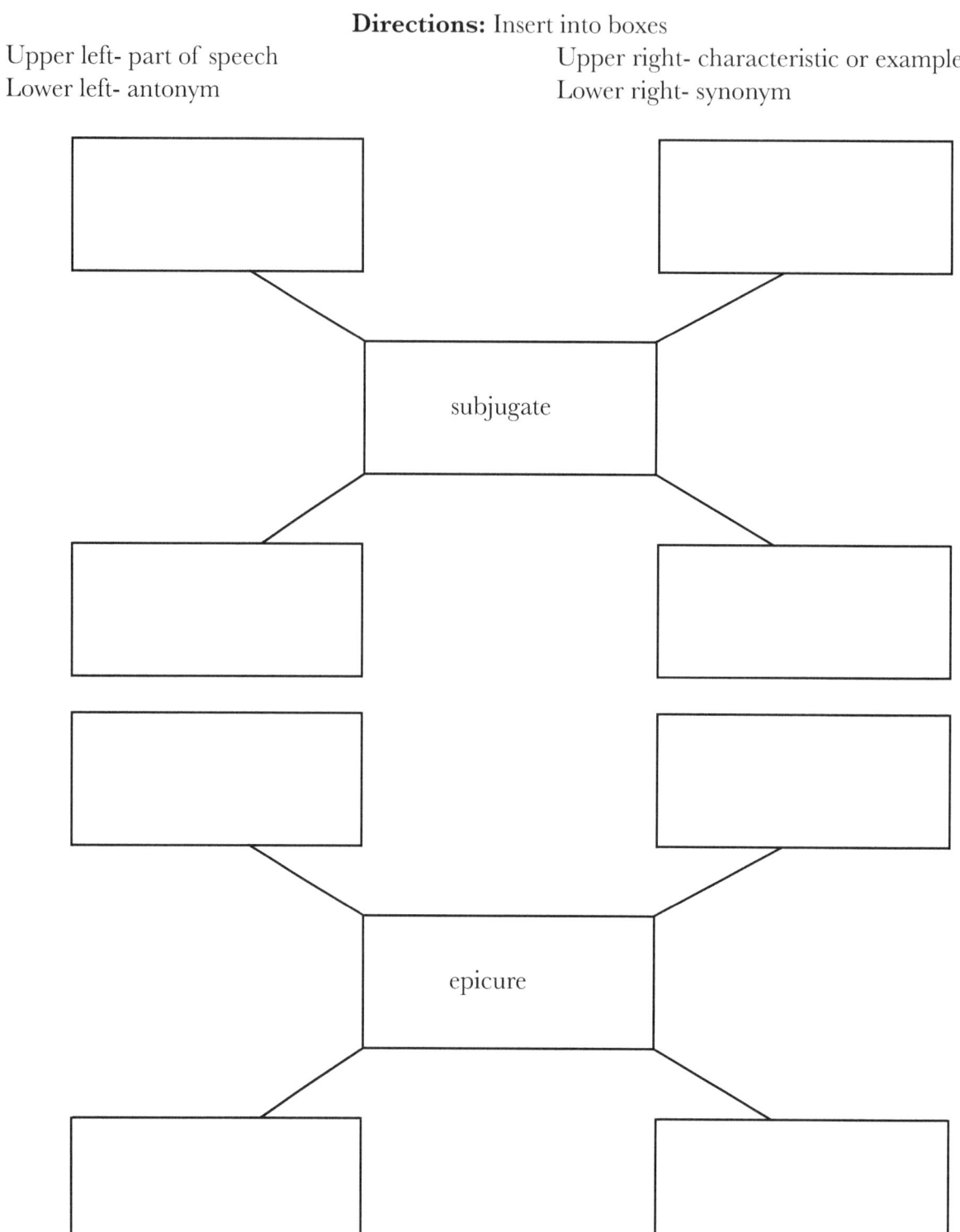

Practice Exercise A

Match the word with the definition:

1. _____ cognitive
2. _____ wit
3. _____ epicure
4. _____ latent
5. _____ amenable
6. _____ perennial
7. _____ astute
8. _____ guttural
9. _____ consensus
10. _____ plagiarism
11. _____ omnipotent
12. _____ panacea
13. _____ secular
14. _____ somatic
15. _____ paragon
16. _____ narcissism
17. _____ introvert
18. _____ sporadic
19. _____ visage
20. _____ subjugate

a. lasting or existing for a long or apparently infinite time; enduring or continually recurring.

b. an exaggerated sense of self-importance, persistent need for admiration, lack of empathy for others, excessive pride in achievements,

c. worldly

d. clever; the ability to reason well

e. a general agreement about something

f. directing feelings to one's own thought and feelings; shy

g. a solution for all ills and difficulties

h. willing to agree or accept

i. an example of excellence and perfection

j. the act or process of knowing

k. relating to the body

l. happening or occurring occasionally

m. the ability to understand things clearly; showing shrewdness

n. throat sounds; being disagreeable and unpleasant

o. the face; slang- your mug

p. having unlimited power; able to do anything

q. to take another's ideas as your own

r. to gain control or obedience by the use of force

s in hidden or dormant form

t. a person who takes particular pleasure in fine food and drink

Practice Exercise B.

(1) Choose five words and write five compound sentences with these words. Write one word per sentence.

1._____
2._____
3._____
4._____
5._____

(2) Choose five words and write five complex sentences with these words. Write one word per sentence.

1._____
2._____
3._____
4._____
5._____

(3) Chose five words and write five compound complex sentences with these words. Write one word per sentence.

1._____
2._____
3._____
4._____
5._____

(4) In complete sentences, define pathos, logos and ethos. Explain the differences between the three.

_____
_____
_____

Chapter 6

Everyday Squares

In this chapter you will learn to:

- Understand the meaning of the words and concepts listed below:

perfunctory	definitive	analogy	culpable
convene	cliché	benevolence	succinct
paradox	concur	gullible	disinclined
recalcitrant	duplicity	segregate	vicarious
redundancy	aesthetic	subjective	peruse

- Know how to use these words in everyday life.

Preview the chapter:

I. Everyday life similarities and differences

II. Using the terms in personal situations

III. Practice Exercises A and B

Define This Chapter's Vocabulary Words

1. _____
2. _____
3. _____
4. _____
5. _____
6. _____
7. _____
8. _____
9. _____
10. _____
11. _____
12. _____
13. _____
14. _____
15. _____
16. _____
17. _____
18. _____
19. _____
20. _____

Introduction

Your everyday life may be filled with lots of activity at times, and at other times things are calm. You may have many problems to solve or you may rely on your parents to solve them for you. But we all know that in our everyday lives, we all act, think and feel in a predictable manner, accepted manner or typical manner. This is normal. But outside of these similarities of thoughts and acts, we do differ somewhat. Some of us live urban lives, while others live rural lives which cause us to think and respond differently. Some of us are athletic, while others find the physical aspects uninteresting and unreachable, underscoring how again, our responses to occurrences in our lives vary. It is the commonalities and differences demonstrated in the examples just mentioned that most of your college professors in your required English and Humanities classes will ask you to write about. And as you write about them, they will ask you to relate them to the assigned readings.

Everyday Squares gives you a chance to learn your target words and practice using them in situations in your everyday life. This means writing definitions, parts of speech, sentences, and scenarios of when you will use these words during your career in college and beyond.

Activity

View the Everyday Square boxes below. Above each box is the targeted word for this chapter. Write the definition in the befinition box, but this time use your own words and not the copied definition from your dictionary. Then write a scenario in which you might use the word. Place this scenario in the scenario box. After writing the scenario, anticipate the response from your listener or reader and write that in the box labeled listener's response. Continue with your Everyday Squares box and write a sentence for the word. Do not use the same sentence you used in your scenario.

Concur

Definition	Scenario
Sentence	Listener's response

Perfunctory

Definition	Scenario
Sentence	Listener's response

Chapter 6: Everyday Squares | 73

Convene

Definition	Scenario
Sentence	Listener's response

Paradox

Definition	Scenario
Sentence	Listener's response

Definitive

Definition	Scenario
Sentence	Listener's response

Cliché

Definition	Scenario
Sentence	Listener's response

Recalcitrant

Definition	Scenario
Sentence	Listener's response

Redundancy

Definition	Scenario
Sentence	Listener's response

Duplicity

Definition	Scenario
Sentence	Listener's response

Peruse

Definition	Scenario
Sentence	Listener's response

Vicarious

Definition	Scenario
Sentence	Listener's response

Succinct

Definition	Scenario
Sentence	Listener's response

Analogy

Definition	Scenario
Sentence	Listener's response

Benevolence

Definition	Scenario
Sentence	Listener's response

Gullible

Definition	Scenario
Sentence	Listener's response

Aesthetic

Definition	Scenario
Sentence	Listener's response

Segregate

Definition	Scenario
Sentence	Listener's response

Culpable

Definition	Scenario
Sentence	Listener's response

Disinclined

Definition	Scenario
Sentence	Listener's response

Subjective

Definition	Scenario
Sentence	Listener's response

Practice Exercise A

Match the word with the definition:

1. _____ concur
2. _____ perfunctory
3. _____ convene
4. _____ paradox
5. _____ definitive
6. _____ cliché
7. _____ recalcitrant
8. _____ redundancy
9. _____ duplicity
10. _____ peruse
11. _____ vicarious
12. _____ succinct
13. _____ analogy
14. _____ benevolence
15. _____ gullible
16. _____ aesthetic
17. _____ segregate
18. _____ culpable
19. _____ disinclined
20. _____ subjective

a. routine; lacking enthusiasm
b. easily persuaded
c. influence by personal feeling
d. a phrase or opinion that is overused
e. unwilling; reluctant
f. deserving blame
g. agree
h. appreciation of beauty
i. the act of kindness
j. to bring together
k. to compare two things for clarity
l. having an uncooperative attitude
m. brief
n. repetition; word and data that can be omitted without loss of meaning
o. read something in a thorough way
p. separate; divide
q. double-dealing; deceitful
r. final
s. statement that is self-contradictory
t. experience through feeling of others

Practice Exercise B

Write several paragraphs about something that happened to you during your life. Write in the first person as though you are with a person, telling him or her the story. Use ten of the terms from this chapter.

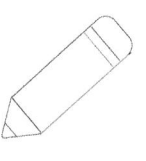

Chapter 7

It Is What It Is

In this chapter you will learn to:

- Understand the meaning of the words and concepts listed below:

abyss	prognosis	malefactor	imperil
herculean	resilient	description	homage
dichotomy	agnostic	irony	mitigate
theory	introvert	imply	proclivity
tortuous	jargon	erudite	profligate

- Know how to use these words in everyday life.

Preview the chapter:

Misused words

Define This Chapter's Vocabulary Words

1. _____
2. _____
3. _____
4. _____
5. _____
6. _____
7. _____
8. _____
9. _____
10. _____
11. _____
12. _____
13. _____
14. _____
15. _____
16. _____
17. _____
18. _____
19. _____
20. _____

Introduction

<u>Misused Words</u>

Sometimes words are misused or confused with other words. At other times, the meaning of a word is not readily understood. In this chapter, you will define the words by stating what they actually mean and what they do not mean. For example, the word *tortuous* is often confused with *torturous*. Tortuous means twisting and winding and torturous means causing pain and anguish. Refer to the chart to see that we explained what it is and what it is not.

tortuous (hint: there is a difference between tortuous and torturous)

Activity

Using a dictionary, define the word in the box labeled, "what it is." Then continue reading the dictionary meaning and write in the box "what it is not," a word or idea that your targeted word can be confused with in usage. If there is no obvious word or idea the word can be confused with, then simply state what it is not. Then using your thesaurus, write the synonym and antonym for the targeted learning word. This first word is done for you.

Tortuous

What it is	What it is not
Something that is twisting and winding such as a path or road.	This word is often confused with torturous because of the similar spelling. Torturous means causing or suffering great pain.
Synonym Twisting; curved	Antonym Straight; direct

Abyss

What it is	What it is not
Synonym	Antonym

Herculean

What it is	What it is not
Synonym	Antonym

Dichotomy

What it is	What it is not
Synonym	Antonym

Theory

What it is	What it is not
Synonym	Antonym

Prognosis

What it is	What it is not
Synonym	Antonym

Resilient

What it is	What it is not
Synonym	Antonym

Agnostic

What it is	What it is not
Synonym	Antonym

Introvert

What it is	What it is not
Synonym	Antonym

Jargon

What it is	What it is not
Synonym	Antonym

Malefactor

What it is	What it is not
Synonym	Antonym

Description

What it is	What it is not
Synonym	Antonym

Irony

What it is	What it is not
Synonym	Antonym

Imply

What it is	What it is not
Synonym	Antonym

Erudite

What it is	What it is not
Synonym	Antonym

Imperil

What it is	What it is not
Synonym	Antonym

Homage

What it is	What it is not
Synonym	Antonym

Mitigate

What it is	What it is not
Synonym	Antonym

Proclivity

What it is	What it is not
Synonym	Antonym

Profligate

What it is	What it is not
Synonym	Antonym

Practice Exercise A

Match the word with the definition:

1. _____ malefactor
2. _____ irony
3. _____ erudite
4. _____ imperil
5. _____ mitigate
6. _____ profligate
7. _____ abyss
8. _____ prognosis
9. _____ herculean
10. _____ resilient
11. _____ dichotomy
12. _____ theory
13. _____ tortuous
14. _____ introvert
15. _____ jargon
16. _____ agnostic
17. _____ description
18. _____ imply
19. _____ proclivity
20. _____ homage

a. wasteful
b. the likely course of a disease or ailment
c. requiring great strength
d. showing great knowledge or learning
e. a spoken or written representation or account of a person object or event
f. deep or bottomless
g. to suggest
h. strong tendency toward something
i. to do wrong; to break the law
j. to show respect
k. able to withstand or recover
l. division between two things
m. to put someone in danger of something
n. shy; inward
o. make less severe
p. complex; twist and turns
q. an event that seems opposite to what one expects; to express something when the opposite is meant
r. slang; words or expressions that belong to a particular profession
s. the existence of God is unknown
t. a probable principle

Practice Exercise B

Go to YouTube and type in: Who's on First? The Sequel with Jimmy Fallon, Billy Crystal and Jerry Seinfeld. Listen to the monologue. Write a response to the monologue. Use a minimum of five words that you have studied in chapters 3 – 7.

(Spoiler Alert: The name of the baseball player on first base is "Who," the name of the baseball player on second base is "What" and the name of the baseball player on third base is "I Don't Know.")

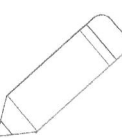

Chapter 8

Taking Words to the Marketplace

In this chapter you will learn to:
- Understand the meaning of the words and concepts listed below:

abridge	scapegoat	deprecate	frivolous
innuendo	biofeedback	pejoratives	transient
charlatan	bucolic	elicit	
presumptuous	capricious	enervate	
denotation	colloquial	feasible	
connotation	delude	flout	

- Develop a unique message about the words to aid in remembering their meaning and usage
- Be able to use the words in college level sentences

Preview of the chapter:

I. Things to look for in a word to help you remember its meaning and usage

   a. history

   b. word parts meanings

   c. country of origin

   d. connotation meanings

II. Where to find information about words

   a. internet   c. dictionary   e. books

   b. thesaurus   d. newspapers   f. professional journals

Define This Chapter's Vocabulary Words

1. _____
2. _____
3. _____
4. _____
5. _____
6. _____
7. _____
8. _____
9. _____
10. _____
11. _____
12. _____
13. _____
14. _____
15. _____
16. _____
17. _____
18. _____
19. _____
20. _____

Introduction

History

Etymology refers to the study of a word's history and country of origin, slang terminology, and how the word was used in the past. Knowing a word's etymology can help you remember the meaning of the word as well as its usage.

Word parts meanings

Word parts refer to the separate bases that are found in words. The smallest unit of a meaning of a word is referred to as a morpheme. All words have at least one morpheme. These separate parts may be the base or root of a word, suffix or prefix. Usually the meanings of all morphemes in a word can help you decipher the meaning of the word. For example, the morpheme "a" means "not" as in "atypical" (not typical).

Country of origin of a word

A way to remember the meaning of a word is to know the word's country of origin. Most words originate because of a country's laws or particular circumstance. Knowing the origin of a word, will most likely "prompt" you to use the word more easily.

Connotative meanings

The connotative meaning is the feeling the word conveys. For example, let's take the word "spring." Most people define "spring" as the second season in the year. However, for many more people, it also means love, sweet smells, or softness. This is the connotative meaning or the feeling the word conveys.

Activity

An entertaining way of learning new words is to be able to associate something funny or interesting about them. In the next exercise, we will "take the words to market" to see if they can be "sold" to buyers. Your buyers will be your mother, father, sister, brother, friend or classmate. The important thing is to know something about the word that is unique, true, interesting, or funny—this will give your word value and determine the worth of your statement.

Ask your parents, father, sister, brother, friends, classmates or grandparents to give you a price on how valuable your statement about the word is worth in order for anyone to remember the meaning. Remember, you may use the history, word parts meanings, country of origin, and/or connotative meaning to create your statement. The best statements are worth five dollars and a good try is worth one dollar.

Prices

$5.00 – great sale; I want it now

$4.00 – good sale; I'll take it by the end of the day

$3.00 – average sale; perhaps I will come back for it

$2.00 – not really interested; good try

$1.00 – no thank you! But since you tried, here is a dollar.

So the question now is, "How do you take a word to market?" Well you need resources and reference material to take your word to market. A dictionary, thesaurus, and sometimes a history book will give you the information you need for your word. What you choose for marketing your word will change from word to word. The point is to pick the most memorable piece of information. The price the purchaser will pay for the word statement depends on how interesting and memorable the information is.

Chapter 8: Taking Words to the Marketplace | 101

Example

$$ sandwich

The term "sandwich" as we know it today is believed to have originated from John Montagu, the 4th Earl of Sandwich, 1762 England. During that period in England, food was served with a piece of meat on the plate, bread on the side and dipping sauce. During a game the 4th Earl of Sandwich ordered that his meal not be separated, but the meat placed between two slices of bread and the sauce in between. Then people started ordering "same as Sandwich," then simply a sandwich.

The current 11th Earl of Sandwich, John Montagu, can trace his peerage to 1625 England.

How much would your parents or friends pay? I got offers of $4.00 - $5.00

Now you take the words to market and sell your word.

$$ abridge

How much would your parents or friends pay?

$$ innuendo

How much would your parents or friends pay?

$$ charlatan

How much would your parents or friends pay?

$$ presumptuous

How much would your parents or friends pay?

$$ denotation

How much would your parents or friends pay?

| $$ connotation |

How much would your parents or friends pay?

| $$ scapegoat |

How much would your parents or friends pay?

| $$ biofeedback |

How much would your parents or friends pay?

$$ bucolic

How much would your parents or friends pay?

$$ capricious

How much would your parents or friends pay?

$$ colloquial

How much would your parents or friends pay?

$$ delude

How much would your parents or friends pay?

$$ deprecate

How much would your parents or friends pay?

$$ pejorative

How much would your parents or friends pay?

$$ elicit

How much would your parents or friends pay?

$$ enervate

How much would your parents or friends pay?

$$ feasible

How much would your parents or friends pay?

Chapter 8: Taking Words to the Marketplace | 107

$$ flout

How much would your parents or friends pay?

$$ frivolous

How much would your parents or friends pay?

$$ transient

How much would your parents or friends pay?

Practice Exercise A

Match the word with the definition:

1. _____ biofeedback
2. _____ bucolic
3. _____ connotation
4. _____ scapegoat
5. _____ capricious
6. _____ feasible
7. _____ flout
8. _____ frivolous
9. _____ transient
10. _____ enervate
11. _____ abridge
12. _____ innuendo
13. _____ elicit
14. _____ charlatan
15. _____ presumptuous
16. _____ denotation
17. _____ colloquial
18. _____ delude
19. _____ pejorative
20. _____ deprecate

a. a way to gain control over involuntary body functions
b. an idea or feeling a word provokes
c. to mislead, deceive or fool
d. to assume without permission; not to observe limits
e. the literal and direct meaning
f. to criticize or disapprove of
g. not having pride or strength
h. a short version of a content that keeps the main sense
i. not formal speech; informal speech
j. to openly disregard, scorn, mock
k. sudden and unpredictable change in attitude, mood, or behavior
l. to bring out a response
m. pleasant country life; countryside aspects
n. occurring only for a short time; a person who is in a place for a short time
o. a person who is blamed of others' wrongdoing
p. no serious value or importance
q. using words to belittle or show disapproval
r. a hint or suggestive remark
s. capable of being accomplished easily
t. fraud; a person claiming to have special knowledge or skills but does not

Practice Exercise B

Write a story about shopping for a personal item. You should use a minimum of 500 words. Use ten terms from this chapter; less than half of your sentences should be simple sentences.

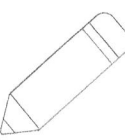

Chapter 9

Writing Analogies

In this chapter you will learn to:

- Understand the meaning of the words and concepts listed below:

incorrigible	bequeath	revoke	inculcate
minutiae	candor	objective	ostracism
taboo	chastise	entrée	prodigious
stereotype	clandestine	ethics	reproach
grievous	validity	flaunt	sardonic

- Learn to compare two words specifically for the purpose of explanation and clarification
- Learn to compare a word to something in order to show significance
- Learn to compare a word to something to prove a point

Preview the chapter:

1. What are analogies and how are they used?
2. Learn to make great analogies.
3. Analogies as a communication tool:
    a. Using analogies for explanation and clarification
    b. Using analogies to show significance
    c. Using analogies to prove a point

Define This Chapter's Vocabulary Words

1. _____
2. _____
3. _____
4. _____
5. _____
6. _____
7. _____
8. _____
9. _____
10. _____
11. _____
12. _____
13. _____
14. _____
15. _____
16. _____
17. _____
18. _____
19. _____
20. _____

Introduction

What are analogies and how are they used?

Analogies are a way to show relationships between words and concepts. Making analogies is a widely used vocabulary technique for college level entry exams. They are also used on many college entrance exams and as an admission tool for some professional programs such as business and nursing.

Before we examine how to use analogies in your writing, we must first examine the different types of relationships used in analogies. Listed below are examples of the popular types of relationships found in analogies.

Example 1 Analogy Relationship Type - opposites
go:stop :: forward:backward. It is read "Go is to stop as forward is to backward."
This analogy shows opposite actions.

Example 2 Analogy Relationship Type - places
Miami:Florida :: Atlanta:Georgia, It is read "Miami is to Florida as Atlanta is to Georgia."
This analogy shows a major city and the state where the city is located.

Example 3 Analogy Relationship Type – Analogy Type - Part Whole
Knee cap: leg :: eyes:head. It is read, "Knee cap is to leg as eyes are to head."
This analogy shows parts of the body that are located on a major (whole) part of the body.

Example 4 Analogy Relationship Type - Cause and Effect
Fire:burn :: freeze:frostbite. It is read, "fire is to burn as freeze is to frostbite."
In this analogy, a fire causes a burn and something frozen (freeze) can cause frostbite.

Example 5 Analogy Relationship Type - synonyms
Nice:likeable :: happy: cheerful. It is read, "Nice is to likeable as happy is to cheerful."
This analogy shows one word definition or description.

Example 6 Analogy Relationship Type - antonym
Pretty:ugly :: run:stop
This one is read pretty is to ugly as run is to stop.
This analogy shows opposites.

As you can see, the key to analogies is finding the same relationship in the first pair of words as in the second. On test and assessments, the first relationship is given and you will have to choose a set that has the same relationship.

Example: Relationship Type - object
Analogy - Bat:ball   Choose the best relationship
1. football:run
2. tennis racket:tennis ball
The best relationship is number two. You use a bat to hit a ball and you use a tennis racket to hit a tennis ball.

Another way analogies are tested is that the first pair is present and the first word of the second pair is present and you will have to find the second word.

Example: Relationship Type - function
Automobiles: drive :: planes:
1. fly
2. wings
The best answer to this analogy is number one fly. You drive automobiles and fly planes. Analogies test three aspects of your vocabulary knowledge: 1) knowing the meaning of words; 2) understanding the relationship of word pairs, and 3) using your inference skills to envision relationships.

Chapter 9: Writing Analogies | 117

Activity

Learn to make great analogies

Use the words from the beginning of this chapter to write analogies using the six relationships. Write *three* analogies for *each* of the 6 different types of analogies: opposites, places, part/whole, cause and effect, synonyms and antonyms.

1. Opposites

_____ : _____ :: _____ : _____

2. Opposites

_____ : _____ :: _____ : _____

3. Opposites

_____ : _____ :: _____ : _____

4. Places

_____ : _____ :: _____ : _____

5. Places

_____ : _____ :: _____ : _____

6. Places

_____ : _____ :: _____ : _____

7. Whole/Part

_____ : _____ :: _____ : _____

8. Whole/Part

_____ : _____ :: _____ : _____

9. Whole/Part

_____ : _____ :: _____ : _____

10. Cause/Effect

_____ : _____ :: _____ : _____

11. Cause/Effect

_____ : _____ :: _____ : _____

12. Cause/Effect

_____ : _____ :: _____ : _____

13. Synonyms

_____ : _____ :: _____ : _____

14. Synonyms

_____ : _____ :: _____ : _____

15. Synonyms

_____ : _____ :: _____ : _____

16. Synonyms

_____ : _____ :: _____ : _____

17. Antonyms

_____ : _____ :: _____ : _____

18. Antonyms

_____ : _____ :: _____ : _____

19. Antonyms

_____ : _____ :: _____ : _____

20. Antonyms

_____ : _____ :: _____ : _____

Analogies as a communication tool

Well, you must be thinking, "analogies are something that I will face on exams, but nobody really uses them." Untrue! We all use analogies in our everyday communications. We use analogies to explain and clarify, to show significance and to prove a point.

Analogies for explanation and clarification

Have you ever had a conversation with someone and that person asked, "What do you mean? I don't get it." Then you simply say, "Well, it's like this." In other words, to explain something you give them a relationship to something else. For example, a friend may ask you how fried alligator tastes. You may give the analogy: fried alligator is like fried chicken. Then the friend may ask, "What if you grill it on the barbeque? You reply, "Then it tastes like grilled chicken." In other words, fried alligator is to fried chicken::grilled alligator is to grilled chicken. You just explained what fried alligator tastes like and allowed your listener to venture into how it will taste if it cooked differently. So you can see, we use analogies in our everyday speech. The use of analogies in writing will only serve to enhance the message you are trying to convey.

Analogies to show significance

How many times have we heard someone use an analogy to show significance? For example, perhaps you heard someone say, "She is walking around here like the Queen of England." Your drivers' education teacher may say, "When traveling 25mph in a car, a direct impact with another car is survivable with your seat belts on; however, when traveling 25mph without a seat belt on, a direct impact with another car may not be survivable."

Writing analogies to prove a point

Sometimes you just want to emphasize a point. You may say, "David's walk to school is like a turtle's walk across the field." The point is that David walks extremely slowly to school. But using an analogy makes the point better than just saying it. Another example of making a point in analogies is if someone ask you if you like noodles and you respond, "Just like I like worms!" This indicates not at all!

From now on, try using analogies in your writing!

Practice Exercise A

Match the word with the definition:

1. _____ incorrigible
2. _____ sardonic
3. _____ minutiae
4. _____ reproach
5. _____ taboo
6. _____ stereotype
7. _____ prodigious
8. _____ grievous
9. _____ ostracism
10. _____ bequeath
11. _____ inculcate
12. _____ revoke
13. _____ candor
14. _____ objective
15. _____ chastise
16. _____ entrée
17. _____ clandestine
18. _____ validity
19. _____ ethics
20. _____ flaunt

a. to teach or instill in someone by repetition or persistence
b. punish usually by beating
c. someone who is not influenced by personal opinion
d. scornful; cynical; bitterly mocking
e. enormous in size, amount, extent, degree, force
f. to call back
g. not able to correct behavior
h. a secret
i. display; show off
j. prohibited or excluded by use, practice or custom
k. to give by will
l. being open, sincere and honest
m. causing great pain or suffering
n. the main course of a meal
o. a small precise detail
p. to express disapproval or disappointment
q. exclusion
r. moral principles
s. a statement of logic and fact
t. a preconceived idea and image about a group of people

Practice Exercise B

Using the vocabulary words from this chapter, write sentences that are analogies, explain, clarify, show significance or make a point.

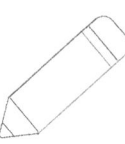

Chapter 10

FANFICTION

In this chapter you will learn to:

- Understand the meaning of the words and concepts listed below:

maladaptive	rhetoric	emporium	implore
fallacy	latent	mimicry	fastidious
peripatetic	neophyte	acrid	gregarious
herculean	genteel	allusion	mercurial
contempt	eminent	dour	perseverance

- Be able to use these words in a fantastic FANFICTION essay

Preview the chapter

I. Multiple meanings of words

II. The writing process

Define This Chapter's Vocabulary Words

1. _____
2. _____
3. _____
4. _____
5. _____
6. _____
7. _____
8. _____
9. _____
10. _____
11. _____
12. _____
13. _____
14. _____
15. _____
16. _____
17. _____
18. _____
19. _____
20. _____

Introduction

You already know that many words in the English language have more than one meaning. When reading a story, the key is to choose the meaning of a word that best fits the context of the writing. Likewise, as a writer, your writing should be so clear that the reader has no doubt as to which meaning you are referring. So take these learning words and write a FANFICTION essay. Remember to have fun with the multiple meanings of the words.
Fanfiction

FANFICTION is taking characters, plots, events, themes, and/or settings from Play Station and X-Box video games, trade books, comic books, You Tube, television, HBO, Netflix, Hulu, Amazon video, REDBOX, popular movies, and/or lyrics to songs and writing a story or essay. You will create your own reality with these characters. The story line does not have to mirror the context of where the character is from. Your FANFICTION should include all the learning words from this chapter.

Now let's get started. Before you begin your essay, let's review the writing process. You probably already know it, but since it is required in college writing classes, it is beneficial to you to start using the writing process now.

The writing process

Brainstorming – on a sheet of paper, write down everything you want to include in your essay. These notes do not need to be in sentences, just phrases and words of ideas. Date your brainstorming.

First Draft- Write the first draft. Review your brainstorming to make sure you included everything. Skip three lines between each sentence when writing this draft. Then reread your essay. Write in notes to strengthen the essay. Date your draft.

Revising- Now get someone to read your draft. Ask them not to respond to grammar, but content. Ask this person to write notes on the content only! The notes should be written on the three lines you skipped.
Ask the person to sign your essay, Revised by_____. Date this revision.

Editing - Rewrite your revision using the suggestions. Again, skip three lines on this rewrite. Then ask a second person to edit it for grammar and sentence usage. Ask the person to sign your essay, Revised by _____. Date this edited version.

Final Draft (Publishing) - Write your final copy using the revision and editing notes. Date this final copy.

Use the blank pages to write your essay using the writing process.

Brainstorming

Date_____

First Draft
Date:_____

Review your work. Strengthen all your sentences.

Revision – Type your first draft and remember to include your notes. Skip three spaces. Print your work. At the end of the page, type "This essay was revised by" _____ and have someone revise (correct for content only) your essay. Ask your reviser to please revise in red or blue or to use track changes. Date your work and label it "revision." Staple your work to this page.

Editing – Use the computer and include all the revision notes. Then edit your work. Ask a colleague to edit your essay again using red or blue and to use track changes. Remember to type on the essay, "Edited by_____." Ask the colleague to sign as the editor. Date your work, print it out and attach/staple your essay to this page.

Publish:

Now type your final copy. Date it and attach it to this page.

Practice Exercise A

Match the word with the definition:

1. _____ fallacy
2. _____ contempt
3. _____ acrid
4. _____ rhetoric
5. _____ latent
6. _____ peripatetic
7. _____ allusion
8. _____ mercurial
9. _____ neophyte
10. _____ maladaptive
11. _____ eminent
12. _____ herculean
13. _____ genteel
14. _____ emporium
15. _____ mimicry
16. _____ fastidious
17. _____ dour
18. _____ gregarious
19. _____ mercurial
20. _____ perseverance

a. not applying adequately
b. traveling from place to place
c. superman; colossal
d. bitter to taste or smell; irritating to the eyes; rough in language or tone
e. open disrespect
f. hidden; not yet developed
g. friendly; sociable
h. continue to do something despite difficulty
i. famous or respect
j. indirect reference
k. demanding; fussy choosy
l. writer or speaker communicates by informing, persuading etc.
m. persistence; determination
n. a large retail store
o. gloomy
p. the act or talent of imitating
q. sociable; found of company
r. polite; respectable
s. sudden or unpredictable changes
t. new to a subject skill or believe

Chapter 11

Voctography: Visualizing Word Meanings

In this chapter you will learn to:

- Understand the meaning of the words and concepts listed below:

placebos	bandanna	noxious	metropolis
sycophant	topography	epitaph	gargantuan
flaccid	idiom	revenge	hover
potpourri	generation	diaphanous	hieroglyphics
taciturn	juxtaposition	horde	

- Present visual representations of the meanings of these words

Preview of the Chapter:

I. How history views the use of pictures to explain complex ideas

    a. English

    b. French

    c. Russian

II. Taking and making pictures

III. Practice exercises A and B

Define This Chapter's Vocabulary Words

1. _____
2. _____
3. _____
4. _____
5. _____
6. _____
7. _____
8. _____
9. _____
10. _____
11. _____
12. _____
13. _____
14. _____
15. _____
16. _____
17. _____
18. _____
19. _____
20. _____

Introduction

How history uses the power of pictures to explain?

The English idiom, "A picture is worth a thousand words," means a complex and multifaceted idea can be communicated with just a picture. The French say, "Un bon croquis vaut mieux qu'un long discours", which was Napoleon Bonaparte's saying, translated in English, "A good sketch is better than a long speech." This notion of substituting visuals for words, sentences, paragraphs and essays is somewhat worldwide. For example, the Russian writer, Ivan Turgenev, wrote in his 1861 novel, *Fathers and Sons*, "The drawing shows me at a glance what might be spread over ten pages in a book." So why bother to write long and extended explanations when a picture will tell all?

Well, in this vocabulary book, you need to do both. So in this chapter, instead of defining terms using your words, use your pictures!

Activity

Below you will find boxes. Draw or take a picture that represents the meaning of the word. If you decide to draw your picture, then use colored pencils or crayons. If you decide to use photos, then use your smartphone or a camera to take the pictures. Paste the pictures in the appropriate box.

Placebo	Bandanna
Topography	Sycophant

Flaccid	Idiom
Generation	Potpourri

Taciturn	Juxtaposition
Metropolis	Noxious

Epitaph	Gargantuan
Hover	Revenge

Diaphanous	Horde
Hieroglyphics	

Practice Exercise A

Match the word with the definition:

1. _____ hieroglyphics
2. _____ noxious
3. _____ gargantuan
4. _____ generation
5. _____ hover
6. _____ juxtaposition
7. _____ idiom
8. _____ epitaph
9. _____ bandanna
10. _____ revenge
11. _____ flaccid
12. _____ diaphanous
13. _____ potpourri
14. _____ sycophant
15. _____ topography
16. _____ placebos
17. _____ taciturn
18. _____ metropolis
19. _____ horde

a. doing something o hurt someone because that person hurt you
b. huge large enormous
c. soft loose flabby
d. a substance that has no effect
e. to hang or suspend in the air
f. two contrasting things placed side by side
g. poisonous; harmful
h. a group of words used often but do not have a literal meaning
i. the capital or key city
j. people born and living at the same time
k. self-seeking; flatterer; leech
l. a large number or group
m. the art of practice or detailing mapping or charting the earth's features
n. writing in memory of a person who died
o. a large handkerchief that is colorful
p. writing using a pictorial character
q. fine and translucent clothe
r. inclined to be silent
s. a mixture of herbs, flowers, and spices that is usually kept in a jar or bowl

Chapter 12

Defining and Poetry

In this chapter you will learn:

- Understand the meaning of the words and concepts listed below:

tryst	epitome	divulge	sarcasm
illicit	condone	elude	judicious
euphemism	conni	elucidate	suppression
tirade	duress	exposition	maudlin
cantankerous	inane	prudent	quintessence

Preview the chapter:

Creative writing using poetry or rap

Define This Chapter's Vocabulary Words

1. _____
2. _____
3. _____
4. _____
5. _____
6. _____
7. _____
8. _____
9. _____
10. _____
11. _____
12. _____
13. _____
14. _____
15. _____
16. _____
17. _____
18. _____
19. _____
20. _____

Introduction

<u>Poetry of Rap</u>

This is your final set of learning words! Define each of these words noting the definition and part of speech. Study these definitions.

Activity

Now that you are finished defining these terms, write a poem or rap that includes these terms. Your poem does not have to rhyme. Write your poem or rap below.

My Poem/ Rap by _____ Date_____

Chapter 12: Defining and Poetry | 151

Practice Exercise A

Match the word with the definition:

1. _____ prudent
2. _____ sarcasm
3. _____ quintessence
4. _____ maudlin
5. _____ tryst
6. _____ illicit
7. _____ euphemism
8. _____ tirade
9. _____ cantankerous
10. _____ epitome
11. _____ condone
12. _____ duress
13. _____ inane
14. _____ divulge
15. _____ elude
16. _____ elucidate
17. _____ exposition
18. _____ judicious
19. _____ suppression
20. _____ connive

a. a perfect and typical example or most concentrated form of class or quality
b. to cooperate secretly, to conspire in secrete to do something immoral, illegal or harmful
c. showing care for the future; avoiding mistakes
d. an explanation; to make clear
e. bad tempered, argumentative, uncooperative
f. a comprehensive expression of a point of view
g. to put to an end
h. a perfect example; a summary of writing
i. to use irony or satire to laugh at someone or something
j. a mild or inoffensive statement in substitution for an offensive statement
k. unlawful
l. secret rendezvous between lovers
m. an angry speech
n. to force someone to do something against their will or better judgment
o. mislead or deceive
p. stupid; silly
q. to accept behavior that is wrong
r. self-pity or foolishly sentimental because of a drunken state
s. sound and good judgment
t. to make known of something that is secret

Bonus Chapter

Foreign Words and Expressions to learn that are "Too Good to Miss"

Foreign Words that are too good to miss

a la carte	caveat emptor	ombudsman
alma mater	cul de sac	status quo
carte blanche	faux pas	verbatim

a la carte: a single item, a separate price   "I know it's cheaper to buy a complete meal but I order ala carte to get everything I really like."

alma mater: an institution where one has graduated, your old school   "I get nostalgic thinking about my alma mater."

carte blanche: complete power to act   "On the way to college, Dad gave me a credit card and said I had carte blanche to make sure I had a good year."

caveat emptor: let the buyer beware   "My realtor said 'caveat emptor' when I wanted to buy the house 'as is'."

cul de sac: a dead end street but also used to express an idea or action that is going nowhere   "I like that my house is on a cul de sac because there is little traffic."

faux pas: a social blunder   "You can imagine my embarrassment when I realized I forgot to remove the price tag from my sweater."

ombudsman: an official who looks into complaints against authorities
"When the dean dismissed the cheating scandal, we informed the ombudsman of the situation."

status quo: the existing or current state of things as they are now "The status quo at the restaurant where I work was below minimum wage. I tried to change that."

verbatim: using the same words "It was as though she had a photographic memory, she recited the story verbatim."

Post Test #1

Circle the best meaning for each word.

1. concur: a. disagree   b. condensed   c. agree   d. conclude

2. delude: a. insane   b. mislead   c. dutiful   d. order

3. enervate: a. weaken   b. enforce   c. strengthen   d. invigorate

4. epitap: a. postscript   b. wrapping   c. greeting card   d. inscription/memorial

5. homage: a. honor/respect   b. ancestral home   c. breakfast food   d. criticize

6. hover: a. surround   b. pause in flight   c. retreat   d. return home

7. illicit: a. insignificant   b. sarcasm   c. permissible   d. unlawful

8. imply: a. expand   b. indicate/suggest   c. provoke/tease   d. dictate

9. maxim: a. proverb/truism   b. greatest amount   c. disorder   d. madness

10. prognosis: a. guarantee   b. venture   c. forecast   d. unwise

11. prudent: a. wise/sensible   b. unwise   c. irritating   d. famous

12. revenge: a. recovery   b. retaliation   c. afterthought   d. proceeds

13. rhetoric: a. speaking/writing   b. puzzle   c. compensation   d. competition

14. scapegoat: a. scandal   b. paranoia   c. mischief maker   d. victim

15. somatic: a. affecting the body   b. leads to an argument   c. tiresome, weary   d. vibrant

16. transient: a. bridge   b. moving around   c. staying   d. interstate

17. tryst: a. engagement   b. rendezvous   c. disturbance   d. business meeting

18. validity: a. truth/fact   b. high ranking student   c. bravery   d. self-praise

19. vicarious: a. indirect/secondhand   b. noticeable   c. essential   d. personal

20. wit: a. support   b. sense of humor   c. charm   d. foolishness

Post Test #2

Circle the best meaning for each word.

1. allusion: a. hint/suggestion   b. accomplice   c. loftiness   d. exact meaning

2. duress: a. duplicate   b. clothing   c. duration   d. force/threat

3. elicit: a. bring forth   b. slander   c. legitimize   d. elect

4. epitome: a. partiality   b. large book   c. model/ideal   d. partiality

5. flaccid: a. large container   b. sudden outburst   c. drooping/inelastic   d. form

6. frivolous: a. worthless/trivial   b. fancy   c. duplicate   d. sensible

7. implore: a. push forward   b. dislike   c. beg/urge   d. demand

8. inculcate: a. elevate   b. diminish   c. teach   d. enjoy

9. jargon: a. specialized language   b. pleasure trip   c. at risk   d. bitterness

10. longevity: a. short period   b. logical thought   c. accommodation   d. life span

11. malefactor: a. wrongdoer/offender   b. kind intentions   c. dangerous situation   d. laziness

12. melancholy: a. many colors   b. indifference   c. cheerful/happy   d. depression/sadness

13. narcissim: a. unworldly person   b. egotistical person   c. bigoted person   d. kind person

14. objective: a. unbiased/impartial   b. prejudicial   c. argumentative   d. death notice

15. placebos: a. pill with no effect   b. physical surroundings   c. metal plaque   d. announcement

16. plagiarism: a. infestation   b. diagram   c. unhappiness   d. copying others work

17. potpourri: a. forcefulness   b. medley/mixture   c. earthenware   d. kettle

18. preposterous: a. captivating   b. absurd/outrageous   c. introduction   d. preparation

19. reproach: a. praise   b. do something again   c. scold   d. hold off

20. secular: a. spiritual/divine   b. worldly/not religious   c. excited   d. sacred

Post Test #3

Circle the best meaning for each word.

1. acrid: a. pungent/sharp   b. hateful   c. indefinite   d. soft/gentle

2. bandana: a. ribbon   b. bangle   c. bandage   d. kerchief/scarf

3. bucolic: a. oversized   b. vegetable   c. countryside   d. distended

4. convene: a. come together   b. speak together   c. contribute   d. dismiss

5. culpable: a. cultivate   b. hostile   c. guilty   d. innocent

6. diaphonous: a. patterned material   b. transparent/sheer   c. cloudy   d. thick fabric

7. discord: a. distribution   b. anxiety   c. harmony   d. dispute

8. etymology: a. study origin of words   b. study moral values   c. study of behavior   d. history courses

9. haphazard: a. controlled   b. complex   c. lively   d. unorganized

10. incorrigible: a. defenseless   b. unruly   c. faultless   d. discomfort

11. introvert: a. withdrawn person   b. worthless person   c. friendly person   d. introduction

12. mercurial: a. planetary exhibition   b. changeable/flighty   c. god of speed   d. stable

13. metropolis: a. cultured place   b. transportation system   c. sophisticated city   d. chief/main city

14. noxious: a. something inconvenient   b. harmful/poisonous   c. fire   d. something useful

15. paradox: a. math term   b. fairy tale   c. self-contradiction   d. maxim

16. paragon: a. lawyer's assistant   b. model/example   c. sorrow   d. puzzle

17. pathos: a. ability to arouse sympathy   b. Greek play   c. garden walk   d. humor

18. recalcitrant: a. contemporary   b. stubborn   c. beneficial   d. compliant

19. redundancy: a. essential   b. payment   c. excess/unnecessary   d. decrease

20. revoke: a. withdraw   b. validate   c. reward   d. repel/disgust

Post Test #4

Circle the best meaning for each word.

1. abyss: a. hateful   b. abusive language   c. entrance   d. bottomless pit

2. aghast: a. sad   b. reciprocate   c. unexcited   d. astonished

3. boon: a. curse   b. bonus, stroke of luck   c. wasteland   d. limitation

4. entrée: a. new arrival   b. entrance/main course   c. admission   d. business tycoon

5. euphemism: a. evangelist   b. funeral speech   c. mild, inoffensive expression   d. compliment

6. exposition: a. display/exhibit   b. enunciation   c. clarification   d. cover-up

7. fallacy: a. fact   b. rejection   c. misconception   d. proficiency

8. intrepid: a. investor   b. fearless/bold   c. invalid   d. cautious

9. latent: a. current   b. newest   c. apparent   d. passive/inactive

10. ostracism: a. shun/snub   b. ancestral home   c. illegal substance   d. inclusive

11. panacea: a. confusion   b. puzzle   c. breakfast food   d. cure-all

12. penury: a. five sided figure   b. five events   c. poverty   d. affluence

13. perennial: a. everlasting   b. able to be seen   c. doing something perfectly   d. perishable

14. perseverance: a. surrender   b. determination   c. prospect   d. lecture

15. subjective: a. inadequate   b. impartial   c. intense   d. personal/emotional

16. succinct: a. to the point   b. substantial   c. effective   d. long winded

17. sycophant: a. spectator   b. parasite/flatterer   c. family member   d. musical instrument

18. taciturn: a. implement   b. routine   c. talkative   d. reserved/aloof

19. tirade: a. long angry speech   b. tiresome   c. parade   d. educational toy

20. tortuous: a. twisting/winding   b. direct   c. painful   d. welcoming

Post Test #5

Circle the best meaning for each word.

1. abridge: a. shorten   b. amplify   c. increase   d. construct

2. amenable: a. energetic   b. passionate   c. compliant   d. uncooperative

3. analogy: a. similarity   b. type of poet   c. outline   d. difference

4. benevolence: a. grief   b. unfriendliness   c. good will   d. worldly goods

5. bequeath: a. plead with   b. hand down/give   c. demonstrate   d. keep/retain

6. candor: a. truthfulness   b. prejudice   c. prankster   d. harmony

7. capricious: a. resistant   b. steady   c. changeable/impulsive   d. constellation

8. consensus: a. twice   b. general agreement   c. difference of opinion   d. nonsense

9. decimate: a. killing every ten   b. decimal system   c. solve   d. break down

10. denotation: a. recommendation   b. markings   c. exact meaning   d. dictionary meaning

11. divulge: a. rotate   b. disclose/reveal   c. differentiate   d. conceal

12. elucidate: a. clarify/explain   b. make perfect   c. narrate   d. confuse

13. genteel: a. refined/courteous   b. sympathetic   c. masculinity   d. considerate

14. gratuitous: a. given without charge   b. necessary   c. uncalled for   d. being grateful

15. gullible: a. worldly   b. easy going   c. easily fooled   d. disinterested

16. horde: a. segments   b. hiding place   c. criminal activity   d. huge number

17. memoirs: a. recalling of past events   b. informal notes   c. trophy   d. awards

18. omniscient: a. helpless   b. can eat everything   c. ability to recall   d. all powerful

19. peripatetic: a. wandering   b. performing   c. puncture   d. abandoned

20. sporadic: a. frivolous   b. very fast   c. irregular/not often   d. continuous

Post Test #6

Circle the best meaning for each word.

1. aesthetic: a. narcissistic   b. painting/artwork   c. appreciation of beauty   d. insensitive

2. agnostic: a. unbeliever   b. entertainer   c. federal agent   d. disciple

3. ambiguity: a. certainty   b. improper   c. inexactness of meaning   d. harmonious

4. dour: a. confident   b. gloomy/sullen   c. reflective   d. cheerful

5. eminent: a. representative   b. high ranking person   c. emperor   d. emblem

6. erudite: a. symbol   b. solemn   c. shallow   d. well informed

7. ethics: a. moral code   b. country of origin   c. religious crusader   d. history course

8. guttural: a. ordinary   b. husky/deep   c. very poor   d. exhaustive

9. herculean: a. cowardly   b. strong/powerful   c. appealing   d. inheritable trait

10. judicious: a. innate   b. stubborn   c. fearless   d. sensible/wise

11. juxtaposition: a. placed side by side   b. morality   c. intersection   d. connection

12. meander: a. go alone   b. go with a purpose   c. go aimlessly   d. go cheerfully

13. minutiae: a. sensation   b. misconduct   c. sentiment/feeling   d. trivia

14. mitigate: a. strengthen   b. relieve/make better   c. update   d. blend

15. perfunctory: a. on time   b. thoughtful   c. disinterested/indifferent   d. sharp minded

16. peruse: a. torment   b. express grief   c. stimulate   d. read

17. proclivity: a. propensity   b. postponing action   c. decency   d. reward

18. sarcasm: a. secret remarks   b. praise   c. witty comments   d. cutting remarks

19. sardonic: a. sarcastic remarks   b. lively remarks   c. embarrassing remarks   d. kind remarks

20. theory: a. truth/fact   b. idea thought to be true   c. period of time   d. verification

Post Test #7

Circle the best meaning for each word.

1. ambivalence: a. clash/conflict   b. industrious   c. generous   d. forgiveness

2. biofeedback: a. memoirs   b. giving feedback   c. ancestry   d. essential dates

3. cognition: a. unfamiliarity   b. awareness/knowledge   c. extension   d. rules

4. colloquial: a. literary   b. intrigue   c. common/everyday   d. huge/vast

5. connive: a. conspire/plot   b. decline   c. rephrase   d. yield

6. definitive: a. inexact   b. complete/reliable   c. respectful   d. honorable

7. deprecate: a. appreciate   b. play down/belittle   c. take from   d. originate

8. dichotomy: a. criticism   b. thickness   c. commitment   d. contrast/differences

9. duplicity: a. something owed   b. uncertainty   c. dishonesty   d. reproduction

10. empathy: a. emphasis   b. approval   c. understand another's feelings   d. equalize

11. emporium: a. shopping mall   b. ancient site   c. empire   d. department store

12. flout: a. steal   b. show contempt   c. show sympathy   d. tearful

13. generation: a. family/offspring   b. thoroughbred   c. aristocrat   d. termination

14. maladaptive: a. kind   b. resentful   c. sickness   d. faulty adaptation

15. maudlin: a. purposeful   b. emotional/sentimental   c. useless   d. old fashioned

16. quintessence: a. classic/epitome   b. five sided figure   c. oddity   d. clever remark

17. resilient: a. rebounding   b. weak   c. inflexible   d. resentful

18. remorseful: a. satisfied   b. agreeable   c. nearby   d. regretful

19. subjugate: a. liberate   b. conquer/subdue   c. raise up   d. under/lower

20. suppression: a. overpower/put down   b. reduction   c. opinion   d. expression

Post Test #8

Circle the best meaning for each word.

1. assumption: a. a belief something is true   b. self-doubt   c. escapade   d. poise

2. charlatan: a. diplomatic person   b. swindler   c. sneaky person   d. king/ruler

3. chastise: a. converse   b. swindle   c. punish/scold   d. gossip/talk idly

4. clandestine: a. secret/hidden   b. revealed   c. family clan   d. fraternal

5. condone: a. punish   b. disapprove   c. encounter   d. ignore/overlook

6. contempt: a. shame/disgrace   b. admiration   c. honor   d. satisfied

7. disinclined: a. insincere   b. objective   c. unwilling   d. enthusiastic

8. imperil: a. endanger   b. defend/save   c. alienate   d. enable

9. inane: a. foolish/senseless   b. worthwhile   c. unaware   d. meaningful

10. innuendo: a. unclear questions   b. hints/suggestions   c. imitation   d. unwanted advice

11. insidious: a. sincere   b. unconcerned   c. devious   d. mysterious

12. mimicry: a. something small   b. imitation   c. small gestures   d. highlights

13. neophyte: a. aristocrat   b. genius   c. rare plant   d. beginner

14. omnipotent: a. unlimited power   b. conquerable   c. impending   d. antiquated

15. profligate: a. profound   b. fabrication   c. wasteful/extravagant   d. upright

16. quixotic: a. unrealistic/idealistic   b. serious   c. materialistic   d. humorous

17. segregate: a. integrate   b. isolate/separate   c. overturn   d. make tense

18. stereotype: a. scoundrel   b. musical instrument   c. typecast/label   d. audience

19. taboos: a. encouraged   b. desired   c. approved   d. something forbidden

20. topography: a. landscape   b. graphic   c. visual/graphic design   d. arranged

Post Test #9

Circle the best meaning for each word.

1. advocate: a. show   b. reciprocate   c. being insensitive   d. recommend

2. apathy: a. self-confidence   b. approval   c. self-government   d. indifference

3. cliché: a. compliment   b. small hat   c. trite phrase   d. group of close friends

4. connotation: a. suggested meaning   b. exact meaning   c. thesaurus meaning   d. opposite

5. description: a. account/portrayal   b. writing   c. downward   d. continuation

6. epicure: a. gourmet   b. delicatessen   c. nutritionist   d. epidemic

7. fastidious: a. charming   b. meticulous   c. intense   d. fearless

8. fortuitous: a. intentional   b. accidental   c. disastrous   d. impressive

9. gargantuan: a. waste material   b. trivial   c. gigantic   d. decoration

10. gregarious: a. sociable/agreeable   b. uninformed   c. immature   d. introverted

11. hieroglyphics: a. wizardry   b. highest point   c. order/ranking   d. ancient writing

12. inductive: a. type of reasoning   b. influence   c. tolerant   d. without doubt

13. infer: a. conclude   b. provoke   c. introduce   d. literal meaning

14. irony: a. sincerity b. double meaning c. disrespect d. anger

15. nonchalant: a. agitated b. unconcerned c. foolishness d. anxious

16. pejorative: a. complimentary b. sympathetic c. admiring d. belittling

17. posthumous: a. after death b. near the back c. descendants d. backyard

18. presumptuous: a. dishonesty b. widespread presence c. belief/guess d. persuasion

19. prodigious: a. profitable b. common/usual c. unholy d. exceptional

20. visage: a. horizon b. preacher c. citizen d. face

Post Test #10

Circle the best meaning for each word.

1. astute: a. gullible b. smart/shrewd c. infamous d. astounding

2. autonomy: a. innovator b. autocrat c. important d. self-government

3. cantankerous: a. kindly/calm b. quarrelsome c. proficient d. lighthearted

4. deductive: a. proper/correct b. definite c. type of reasoning d. battered

5. elude: a. lengthen b. avoid/escape c. extend d. eligible

6. feasible: a. likely to happen b. impossible c. large feast d. effective

7. flaunt: a. conceal b. quick departure c. show off d. avoid

8. grievous: a. trivial b. sad/tragic c. selfish d. indifferent

9. idiom: a. phrase/expression b. foolishness c. philosophy d. illiteracy

10. inhibition: a. holding back b. inheritance c. imagination d. wrongdoing

11. jocularity: a. sportsman b. jovial person c. judge d. author

12. logos: a. reasoning b. logical statement c. unlikely d. emblem/symbol

13. ethos: a. original b. praise c. ethics/morals d. ethnicity

Answer Key

Answer Key for Post Test

Post Test #1
1. c   2. b   3. c   4. d   5. a   6. b   7. d   8. b   9. a   10. c   11. a   12. b   13. a
14. d   15. a   16. b   17. b   18. a   19. a   20. b

Post Test #2
1. a   2. d   3. a   4. c   5. c   6. a   7. c   8. c   9. a   10. d   11. a   12. d
13. b   14. a   15. a   16. d   17. b   18. b   19. c   20. b

Post Test #3
1. a   2. d   3. c   4. a   5. c   6. b   7. d   8. a   9. d   10. b   11. a   12. b
13. c   14. b   15. c   16. b   17. a   18. b   19. c   20. a

Post Test #4
1. d   2. d   3. b   4. b   5. c   6. a   7. c   8. b   9. d   10. a   11. d   12. b   13. a
14. b   15. d   16. a   17. b   18. d   19. a   20. a

Post Test #5
1. a   2. c   3. a   4. c   5. b   6. a   7. c   8. b   9. a   10. d   11. b   12. a   13. a
14. a   15. c   16. d   17. a   18. d   19. a   20. c

Post Test #6
1. c   2. a   3. b   4. b   5. b   6. d   7. a   8. b   9. B   10. d   11. a   12. c
13. d   14. b   15. c   16. d   17. a   18. d   19. a   20. b

Post Test #7
1. a   2. b   3. b   4. c   5. a   6. b   7. b   8. d   9. c   10. c   11. d   12. b   13. a
14. d   15. b   16. a   17. a   18. d   19. b   20. a

Post Test #8
1. a   2. b   3. c   4. a   5. d   6. a   7. c   8. a   9. a   10. b   11. c   12. b   13. d
14. a   15. c   16. a   17. b   18. c   19. d   20. a

Post Test #9
1. d   2. d   3. c   4. a   5. a   6. a   7. b   8. b   9. b   10. a   11. d   12. a   13. a
14. b   15. b   15. b   16. d   17. a   18. c   19. d   20. d

Post Test #10
1. b   2. d   3. b   4. c   5. b   6. a   7. c   8. b   9. a   10. a   11. b   12. d   13. c

Answer Key for Chapters 1 - 12

Chapter 1: Those Phrases and Clauses

Practice Exercise I- Test your knowledge on prepositions. Without looking back at the list of propositions, write in the boxes of the matrix all the prepositions you can remember.

Answer: Students should fill in the boxes with prepositions. Students may use propositions that are not on the list.

Practice Exercise 2 – Look back at the paragraph on "A Paint Ball Game. List in the space providing all the prepositions found in the paragraph.

Answer:

In	to	without
If	by	with
On	of	without

Practice Exercise 3 – Build the simple sentence. Give the sentences below a direct and active meaning by adding a preposition or prepositional phrase.

Answers:

a) given in as another example

b) Since I like to listen to music on my lunch breaks, my coworkers gave me a permanent seat by the electrical socket. [or something similar]

c) My home is around the corner so it will be easy for you to find. [or something similar]

d) Among the ruins, I found a doll. [or something similar]

e) As I said earlier, time is slipping by.

Practice Exercise 4- In the earlier selection on "A Paint Ball Game", try to find the participial phrase and write them below.

Answers:

<u>Feeling the whistling noise</u>   <u>targeting another body frame</u>   <u>realizing that they would recover</u>

Practice Exercise 5 - Find five infinitives in "A Paint Ball Game."
Answers:

<u>To fire</u>   <u>to win</u>   <u>to gain</u>   <u>to leave</u>   <u>to continue</u>

Practice Exercise 6 - Underline the phrases in the following sentences. Then on the line beneath the sentence identify the type of phrase: prepositional, participial or infinitive phrase.

1. <u>To get</u> better grades, he studied more.
<u>Infinitive phrase</u>

2. We work <u>to earn</u> a living.
<u>Infinitive phrase</u>

3. I love cooking meals <u>for us.</u>
<u>Prepositional phrase</u>

4. The children fled the old house, <u>screaming that they had seen a ghost</u>.
<u>Participial phrase</u>

5. His picture hangs <u>above the fireplace</u>.
<u>Prepositional phrase</u>

6. <u>Without her help</u>, we would have been lost.
<u>Prepositional phrase</u>

7. <u>Because of his kindness and consideration</u>, he won the scholarship.
<u>Prepositional phrase</u>

8. He works hard to earn a better salary and <u>to support</u> his family.
<u>Prepositional phrases</u>

9. Practicing all day long, helped him earn a spot <u>on the football team</u>.
<u>Participial phrase and prepositional phrase</u>

10. My sister is the girl <u>wearing a pink suit</u>.
<u>Participial phrase</u>

11. <u>As soon</u> as it got dark, they went home.
<u>Prepositional phrase</u>

12. I love cooking meals <u>for us.</u>
<u>Prepositional phrase</u>

13. He works hard to earn a better salary.

Infinitive phrase

14. His picture hangs above the fireplace.

Prepositional phrase

15. She threw the ball at me.

Prepositional phrase

16. You can see the pain on the old man's face from working all day long.

Prepositional phrase and participial phrase

17. His participating here has helped many children learn the importance of good health.

Participial phrase and prepositional phrase

18. Jogging to work helped Diana stay healthy.

Participial phrase

19. He loves to sing in the shower.

Prepositional phrase

20. Dancing all night long caused the young student to oversleep.

Participial phrase and infinitive phrase

Practice Exercise 7 – Below are dependent clauses (DC). They are prepositional phrases, participial phrases and infinitive phrases. In front of the dependent clause (DC), write an independent clause (IC) to make the clause into a sentence.

Answers

1. until we meet again

Sentence: I will keep your scarf until we meet again.

2. to run

Sentence: I like to run.

3. singing in the shower

Sentence: My father is always singing in the shower.

Practice exercise 8 - In the following sentences, mark the underlined groups of words as IC for independent clause or DC for dependent clause.

Answers:

1. <u>We listened to music</u> while we drove home. IC
2. <u>As soon as it was dark</u>, they went home. DC
3. If we get up early enough, <u>we will be able to watch the sunrise</u>. IC
4. They work hard <u>so that they may party well</u>. DC
5. Whenever I hear her voice, <u>I think of home</u>. DC
6. Mary went to the dance <u>because she wanted to meet her best friend</u>. DC
7. The weather was warm <u>during the night</u>. DC
8. The teacher was tired <u>so she gave the students seat assignments.</u> DC
9. Martha got a new car <u>since the old one continuously broke down on her</u>. DC
10. <u>We went to all the stores</u> trying to find the dress. IC

Chapter 2: Writing Awesome Sentences and Speaking Like a College Student

Exercise 1: Write three simple sentences and point to the subject and underline the verb.

Answers

Sentences will vary.

Exercise 2: Combine the two sentences below making them into a compound sentence.

Answers: Coordinating conjunctions (FANBOYS) and the semi colon may vary.

1. Alice did not particularly care for the salad dressing offered.
    She made another choice.

Compound sentence: Alice did not particularly care for the salad dressing offered, so she made another choice.

2. Those who knew him said he was reserved.
    He introduced himself to everyone at the party.

Compound sentence: Those who knew him said he was reserved, but he introduced himself to everyone at the party.

3. George can buy new skis during the summer sales.

   He can polish his old ones and use them or another year.

Compound sentence: George can buy new skis during the summer sales, or he can polish his old ones and use them or another year.

4. He's a jolly good fellow.

   He's a jolly good fellow.

Compound sentence: He's a jolly good fellow; he's a jolly good fellow.

5. Marie never fully accepted the gravity of her father's condition.

   Did she grasp his illness as a terminal one.

Compound sentence: Marie never fully accepted the gravity of her father's condition, nor did she grasp his illness as a terminal one.

6. John hasn't called in sick.

We are quite worried about him.

Compound sentence: John hasn't called in sick; we are quite worried about him.

7. I studied hard for the exam.

I received a very high grade.

Compound sentence: I studied hard for the exam, and I received a very high grade.

8. Steve plays the saxophone.

May sings folk songs.

Compound sentence: Steve plays the saxophone, and May sings folk songs.

9. The sun was shining.

It was raining.

Compound sentence: The sun was shining, yet it was raining.

10. Larry is the best player on the team.

He was ill the day of the big game.

Compound sentence: Larry is the best player on the team, he was ill the day of the big game.

11. The final was scheduled for today.

The professor is absent.

Compound sentence: The final was scheduled for today, but the professor is absent.

12. The nurse gave the child some medicine.

It was delicious.

Compound sentence: The nurse gave the child some medicine, and it was delicious.

13. Bertha loves Clint Eastwood.

She goes to all of his movies.

Compound sentence: Bertha loves Clint Eastwood; she goes to all of his movies.

14. Sue cleaned the boat.

Mike secured the rigging.

Compound sentence: Sue cleaned the boat; Mike secured the rigging.

15. George was playing the tuba.

Mary was not listening.

Compound sentence: George was playing the tuba, Mary was not listening.

Exercise 3 – Read the two independent clauses below. Change one of the independent clauses into a dependent clause (prepositional phrase, participial phrase or infinitive phrase) and then write a complex sentence. Answers may vary.

1. It was raining.

The sun was shining brightly.

Complex sentence: Although it was raining, the sun was shining brightly.

2. I finished working.

I took a nap.

Complex sentence: Since I finished working, I took a nap.

3. Mark has a fever.

Please don't visit him.

Complex sentence: Please don't visit Mark because he has a fever.

Answer Key

4. Let's light the fireplace.

It's cold tonight.

Complex sentence: Let's light the fire place because it is cold tonight.

5. The teacher would not leave.

The last child left.

Complex sentence: The teacher would not leave until the last child left.

6. It is raining.

The children have umbrellas.

Complex sentence: Because it is raining outside, the children have umbrellas.

7. The boys are in the park.

Their parents are at work.

Complex sentence: Although their parents are at work, the boys are in the park.

8. People used more fuel than usual.

It was the coldest winter in a century.

Complex sentence: During the coldest winter in the century, people used more fuel than usual.

9. The famous singer sang his most popular songs.

Thousands of people applauded.

Complex sentence: As the famous singer sang his most popular songs, thousands of people applauded.

10. Mary won't show up.

John says so.

Complex sentence: Mary won't show up until John says so.

11. People are happy.

The stock market is going up.

Complex sentence: Because the stock market is going up, people are happy.

12. We watched.

The sky turned gray.

Complex sentence: As we watched, the sky turned gray.

13. Her mother took the doll.

The little girl cried.

Complex sentence: The little girl cried after her mother took the doll.

14. We worked on the car.

The girls watched TV.

Complex sentence: As we worked on the car, the girls watched TV.

15. I went to see "Hamilton."

I became a big fan of the theatre.

Complex sentence: After I went to see Hamilton, I became a big fan of the theatre.

Now write three complex sentences on your own.

1. sentences vary

2. sentences vary

3. sentences vary

Exercise 4 - Using commas, FANBOYS and semicolons as appropriate, combine the following groups of simple sentences into compound complex sentences. Remember to place a comma before your coordinating conjunctions (FANBOYS) and a comma after the dependent clause. The first sentence is done for you.

1. It was Friday the thirteenth.

Margaret was scared all day.

Bob scoffed at the silly superstitions of his friends.

Compound Complex sentence: Because it was Friday the thirteenth, Margaret was scared all day, but Bob scoffed at the silly superstitions of his friends.

2. Winter snow in the Rockies gets very deep.

Avoiding snow drifts becomes imperative.

One must exercise caution.

Compound Complex sentence: Avoiding the snow drifts becomes imperative, since winter in the Rockies gets very deep, and one must exercise caution.

3. Joe bought a new car.

He had brake problems the week after he purchased it.

He was furious.

Compound Complex sentence: Joe bought a new car, but he had brake problems the week after he purchased it, which made him furious.

4. The baby cried steadily.

His mother came home.

The babysitter heaved a sigh of relief.

Complex Compound sentence: The baby cried steadily until the mother came home,

5. We go to Knottsberry Farm.

We want delicious and fresh strawberries.

We pick the fruit to our hearts' content.

Compound Complex sentence: Since we want delicious and fresh strawberries, we go to Knottsberry Farm, so we pick the fruit to our hearts' content.

6. John runs.

He drinks Gatorade.

He does warm up exercises.

Compound Complex sentence: John drinks Gatorade because he runs and does warm up exercises.

7. You want to pick up your paycheck.

You must come to the office on the fifth floor.

Proper identification must be presented.

Compound Complex sentence: If you want to pick up your paycheck, you must come to the office on the fifth floor, and proper identification must be presented.

8. Jill leaves.

I will call you.

Don't wait up for or my call.

Compound Complex sentence: After Jill leaves, I will call you; don't wait up for my call.

9. Gloria enjoys playing tennis.

She rarely has time for the sport.
She is carrying a full course load at the university.
Compound Complex sentence: Gloria enjoys playing tennis, but she rarely has time for the sport because she is carrying a full course load at the university.

10. It rained so much.
The pond behind our house overflowed.
Our kitchen floor was damaged.
Compound Complex sentence: It rained so much that the pond behind our house overflowed, resulting in our kitchen floor being damaged.

11. I will not give you any apple pie.
You eat every bit of your dinner.
I mean what I say.
Compound Complex sentence: I will not give you any apple pie before you eat every bit of your dinner, and I mean what I say.

12. Miguel had a strong personality.
Everyone in the village liked him.
He was frequently called upon to settle disputes.
Compound Complex sentence: Since Miguel had a strong personality, everyone in the village liked him, and he was frequently called upon to settle disputes.

13. Douglas treads.
No man dares to walk.
He frequently gets into trouble.
Compound Complex sentence: Frequently getting into trouble, Douglas treads; no man dares to walk.

14. You begin the College Entrance Exam.
Please put your name in the boxes at the top of the page.
Read the directions very carefully.
Compound Complex sentence: As you begin the College Entrance Exam, please put your name in the boxes at the top of the page, and read the directions very carefully.

15. Shooting deer is not one of Bill's favorite sports.

He thought of declining the invitation.

He heard most of his friends would participate in the hunting expedition.

Compound Complex: Because shooting deer is not one of Bill's favorite sports, he thought of declining the invitation, but he heard most of his friends would participate in the hunting expedition.

Now you write three compound complex sentences on your own.

1. sentence vary

2. sentence vary

3. sentence vary

Chapter 3 Analyze a Word

Exercise A

1. g
2. e
3. f
4. h
5. k
6. a
7. i
8. j
9. l
10. c
11. t
12. q
13. s
14. b
15. n
16. p
17. m
18. r
19. o
20. d

Exercise B

Sentences will vary.

Chapter 4 Painting Words

Exercise A

1. g	11. d
2. m	12. e
3. i	13. o
4. p	14. h
5. n	15. j
6. q	16. k
7. a	17. t
8. c	18. r
9. b	19. l
10. s	20. f

Exercise B

Sentences will vary

Chapter 5 Mapping Words

Exercise A

1. j	11. p
2. d	12. g
3. t	13. c
4. s	14. k
5. h	15. i
6. a	16. b
7. m	17. f
8. n	18. l
9. e	19. o
10. q	20. r

Practice Exercise B

Sentences will vary for exercises 1 – 3.

In exercise 4 the correct (dictionary) meaning of pathos, logos and ethos with a statement of the differences.

Chapter 6 Everyday Squares

Exercise A

1. g
2. a
3. j
4. s
5. r
6. d
7. l
8. n
9. q
10. o
11. t
12. m
13. k
14. i
15. b
16. h
17. p
18. f
19. e
20. c

Exercise B

Paragraphs will vary.

Chapter 7 It Is What It Is

Exercise A

1. i
2. q
3. d
4. m
5. o
6. a
7. f
8. b
9. c
10. k
11. l
12. t
13. p
14. n
15. r
16. s
17. e
18. g
19. h
20. j

Exercise B

Responses will vary.

Chapter 8 Words to the Marketplace

Exercise A
1. a
2. m
3. b
4. o
5. k
6. s
7. j
8. p
9. n
10. g
11. h
12. r
13. l
14. t
15. d
16. e
17. i
18. c
19. q
20. f

Exercise B
Answers will vary

Chapter 9 Writing Analogies

Exercise A
1. g
2. d
3. o
4. p
5. j
6. t
7. e
8. m
9. q
10. k
11. a
12. f
13. l
14. c
15. b
16. n
17. h
18. s
19. r
20. i

Practice Exercise B
Sentences will vary.

Chapter 10 FANFICTION

Exercise A

1. a
2. e
3. d
4. l
5. f
6. b
7. j
8. s
9. t
10. a
11. i
12. c
13. r
14. n
15. p
16. k
17. o
18. g
19. h
20. m

Exercise B

Essay: Brainstorming notes; Draft hand written; Revision typed with revised by signature and attached; Edit typed with edited by; Publish – typed and attached.

Chapter 11 Voctography: Visualizing Word Meanings

Exercise A

1. p
2. g
3. b
4. j
5. e
6. f
7. h
8. n
9. o
10. a
11. c
12. q
13. s
14. k
15. m
16. d
17. r
18. i
19. l

Chapter 12 Defining and Poetry

Exercise A

1. c
2. i
3. a
4. r
5. l
6. k
7. j
8. m
9. e
10. h
11. q
12. n
13. p
14. t
15. o
16. d
17. f
18. s
19. g
20. b

Academic Vocabulary Words

The Big 205

abridge ch 8
abyss ch 7
acrid ch 10
advocate ch 4
aesthetic ch 6
aghast ch 4
advocate ch 4
agnostic ch 7
allusion ch 10
ambiguity ch 4
ambivalence ch 4
amenable ch 5
analogy ch 6
apathy ch 3
assumption ch 3
astute ch 5
autonomy ch 3
bandanna ch 11
benevolence ch 3, 6
bequeath ch 9
biofeedback ch 3, 8
boon ch 4
bucolic ch 8
candor ch 9
cantankerous ch 12
capricious ch 8
charlatan ch 8
chastise ch 9
clandestine ch 9
cliche' ch 6
cognition ch 5
colloquial ch 8
concur ch 6
condone ch 12
connive ch 12
connotation ch 8
consensus ch 5

contempt ch 10
convene ch 6
culpable ch 6
decimate ch 3
deductive ch 3
definitive ch 6
delude ch 8
denotation ch 8
deprecate ch 8
description ch 7
diaphanous ch 11
dichotomy ch 6
discord ch 4
description ch 7
disinclined ch 6
divulge ch 12
dour ch 10
duplicity ch 6
duress ch 12
elicit ch 8
elucidate ch 12
elude ch 12
empathy ch 3
eminent ch 10
emporium ch 10
enervate ch 8
entrée ch 9
epicure ch 5
epitaph ch 11
epitome ch 12
erudite ch 7
ethics ch 9
ethos ch 5
etymology ch 3
euphemism ch 12
exposition ch 12
fallacy ch 10

fastidious ch 10
feasible ch 8
flaccid ch 11
flaunt ch 4, 9
flout ch 8
fortuitous ch 3
frivolous ch 8
gargantuan ch 11
generation ch 11
genteel ch 10
gratuitous ch 3
gregarious ch 10
grievous ch 9
gullible ch 6
guttural ch 5
haphazard ch 4
herculean ch 7, 10
hieroglyphics ch 11
homage ch 7
horde ch 11
hover ch 11
idiom ch 11
illicit ch 12
imperil ch 7
implore ch 10
imply ch 7
inane ch 12
incorrigible ch 9
inculcate ch 9
inductive ch 3
infer ch 4
inhibition ch 3
innuendo ch 8
insidious ch 4
intrepid ch 4
introvert ch 5, 7
irony ch 7

jargon ch 7
jocularity ch 3
judicious ch 12
juxtaposition ch 11
latent ch 5, 10
longevity ch 4
logos ch 5
maladaptive ch 10
malefactor ch 7
maudlin ch 12
maxim ch 3
meander ch 4
melancholy ch 4
memoirs ch 3
mercurial ch 10
metropolis ch 11
mimicry ch 10
minutiae ch 4, 9
mitigate ch 7
narcissism ch 5
neophyte ch 10
nonchalant ch 4
noxious ch 11
objective ch 9
omnipotent ch 3,5
omniscient ch 3
ostracism ch 9
panacea ch 5
paradox ch 6
paragon ch 5
pathos ch 5
pejorative ch 8
penury ch 4
perennial ch 5
perfunctory ch 6
peripatetic ch 10
perseverance ch 10

peruse ch 6
placebos ch 11
plagiarism ch 5
posthumous ch 3
potpourri ch 11
preposterous ch 4
presumptuous ch 8
proclivity ch 7
prodigious ch 9
profligate ch 7
prognosis ch 7
prudent ch 12
quintessence ch 12
quixotic ch 4
recalcitrant ch 6
redundancy ch 6
remorseful ch 4
reproach ch 9
resilient ch 7
revenge ch 11
revoke ch 9
rhetoric ch 10
sarcasm ch 12
sardonic ch 9
scapegoat ch 8
secular ch 5
segregate ch 6
somatic ch 5
sporadic ch 5
stereotype ch 9
subjective ch 6
subjugate ch 5
succinct ch 6
suppression ch 12
sycophant ch 11
taboos ch 9
taciturn ch 11

theory ch 7
tirade ch 12
topography ch 11
tortuous ch 7
transient ch 3, 8
tryst ch 12
validity ch 9
vicarious ch 6
visage ch 5
wit ch 5

Foreign Words that are too good to miss
a la carte
caveat emptor
ombudsman
alma mater
cul de sac
status quo
carte blanche
faux pas
verbatim

About the Authors

Patsy Trand, Ph.D., is a faculty member of Florida International University and the former administrator of the FIU Reading and Learning Lab. Dr. Trand teaches undergraduate, honors, and graduate courses for the FIU School of Arts and Sciences. She is committed to passing on her wealth of knowledge and experience to help high school and college students reach their academic goals. She has authored many articles and has presented at many national and international conferences.

Kay Lopate, Ph.D., is a Professor Emeritus from the University of Miami, Miami, Florida where she co-founded the Reading and Study Skills Center and taught for the School of Education. Her special interests are preparing PreMed students for medical school and helping undergraduates acquire advanced reading ability to succeed in the demands of mastering college level texts.

Congratulations for completing "Vocabulary university professors say all college students should know."

Your speaking and writing vocabularies create a self-portrait of who you are--and it's true that people judge you by the words you use. It's also true that a large vocabulary allows you to understand the thoughts and ideas that others express through their words.

We hope that learning (and using) the Big 205 words will encourage you to keep expanding your vocabulary. We also hope that you will use your newly learned words when speaking and writing.

Patsy Trand, Ph.D. Kay Lopate, Ph.D.

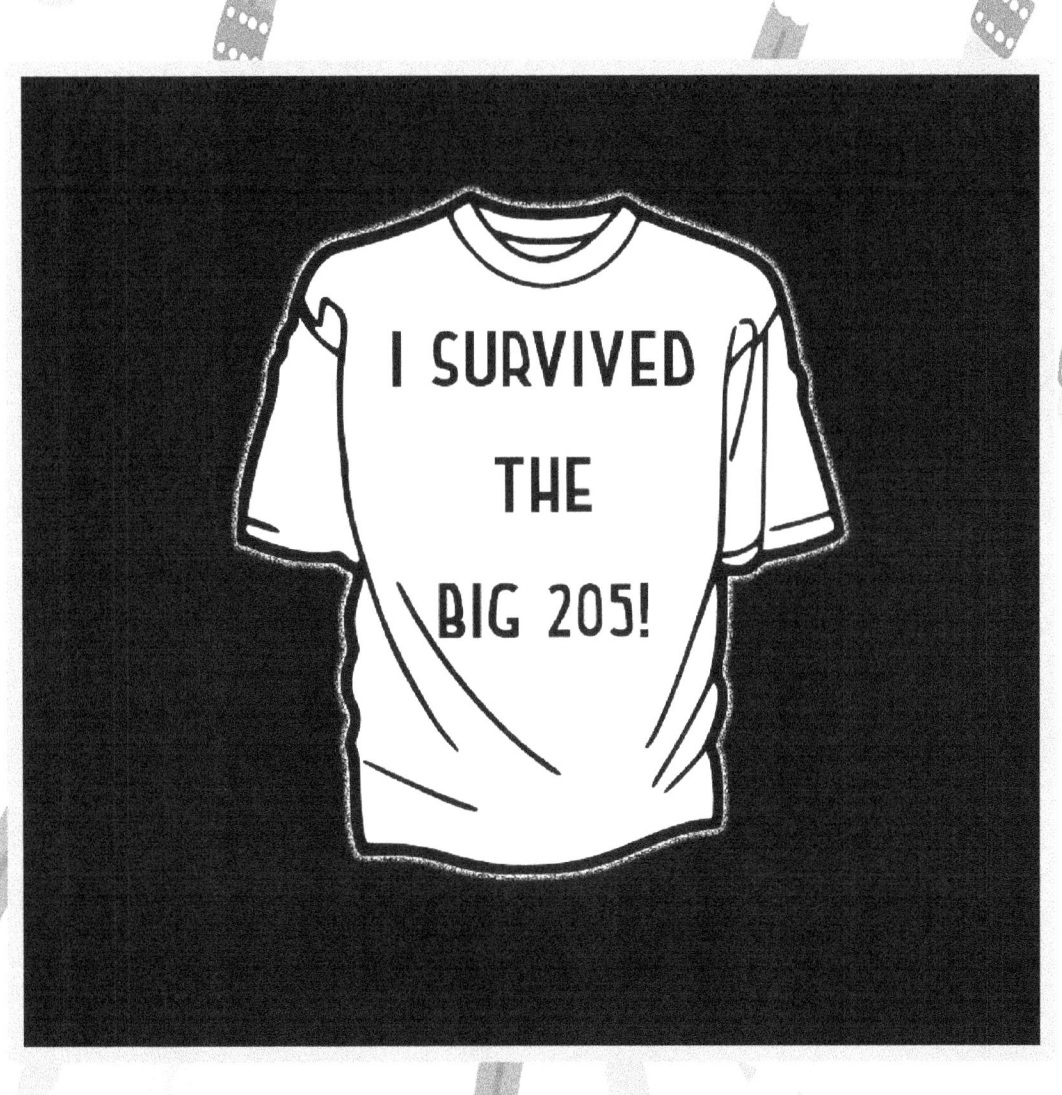

www.ingramcontent.com/pod-product-compliance
Lightning Source LLC
Chambersburg PA
CBHW060313240426
43661CB00059B/2751